Little Old Lady Alone

L.O.L.A.

Read All About It

Heti Davies

FOR Sue and Ian.
Love ~ Best wishes
Heti

Pen Press

First published in Great Britain by Pen Press

ISBN 978-1-906206-91-8

Printed and bound in the UK by Cpod, Trowbridge, Wiltshire
Pen Press is an Imprint of Indepenpress Publishing Ltd
25 Eastern Place
Brighton
BN2 1GJ

A catalogue record of this book is available from
the British Library

Cover design by Jacqueline Abromeit

Also by Heti Davies

Numerous writings, composed with much hilarity after midnight and dispatched next day to the City landfill sites.

For Me

"TI WYDDOST BETH DDYWED FY NGHALON"

Thanks

…to all who have laughed at my writings and to those who have cried.

The One Big Thank You is to my friend and colleague, Dr William McCrea who has encouraged and supported me in everything at every stage.

Disclaimer

The views contained in this book are those of the author and believed to be unreliable and inaccurate.

No liability is accepted at any time for anything about anything.

The author is not authorised or regulated by any Authority.

ALL the characters in this book are fashioned on friends and colleagues who are extravagantly misquoted.

You will recognise yourselves.

And you will be understanding because
       I am a LOLA
       I can't remember and/or choose to forget.

P.S. You could SUE. It would be fun.

Contents

FUN (EVEN FROLICS) AT "THE FRINGE" FOR FEMALE AGE 76 ¾ – ALONE

Ideally you should observe important Rules and Guidelines – some obvious, some more subtle. Like: Never apologise for your age, instead, capitalise on your age, over 70 is an advantage, jump the queue – in a confused way, sit down anywhere – indicate you are having a "senior moment", get a man (any man) to hail a taxi for you. They don't stop for a LOLA (Little Old Lady Alone).

Motto is Be Prepared. Beforehand, take a whole weekend to study the brochure – armed with highlighters and your favourite tipple. First check what is free, scour all previews, all BBC shows and then hang around the venues for give away tickets.

Next – Make a month's Calendar of Events and spread it out on the dining table (you won't need the table as you'll be out at shows or grabbing a sandwich or hopefully just a dry white).

Choose a Cross-Section. Comedy/Theatre/Exhibition etc.

I recommend:

1. Something classical – preferably Greek and preferably at "The Traverse".
2. Something with "SEX" in the title – pretend you don't understand.
3. One show which includes NUDITY is de rigeur – queue early, sit in the front and take notes or memorise every detail – useful for dinner party talk during the winter.
4. Any play about DEATH – laugh loudly or sit impassively. This makes others and the cast uncomfortable and that's great fun.

5. Something at an unusual venue but not if it's a car or telephone booth or lavatory.

This brings me to the problem of venues.

Try to concentrate on one main venue per day. You will look silly running at your age up to The Pleasance – you might just expire – remember you are a LOLA.

I am assuming that being 76¾ and female you have at least one affliction from the following two groups:

Group A: Impaired eyesight/hearing or mobility/breathlessness/dizziness/anxiety.

Group B: Bladder problems.

So – inspect the venues regarding:

STEPS – avoid 5 storeys up or treacherous basements.

A TORCH is handy – there are many underground passages and locate ALL TOILETS EVERYWHERE. (Most of you will be on water tablets, so decide the night before when exactly to take your tablet – if necessary, wait until you get home at midnight and stay awake all night.)

SEATS AT SHOWS – choose carefully. I advise the back row for classical and snoozing, the middle rows if you intend leaving during the performance and the front rows for anything risqué.

If picked upon by the comedian, do give your correct name and occupation as there will surely be someone there who knows you. However, if you are a landlady, lap dancer, reflexologist, theatre critic or psychiatrist, it's wiser to lie or stay at the back or stay at home.

Regarding clothes, anything goes. Just for fun and research, I do one day posh and drink wine and meet a friend between shows and next day dowdy and dubious and eat in the queue.

All the Fringe frolicking takes money – remember you can do 30 or more events for the price of a couple of main Festival evenings.

And remember there are perks of being 76¾ and of being alone. You can avoid the shows you hate, you can relax, leave half way, talk to strangers, drink and eat when, what and how much you like and be eccentric; and if the whole thing becomes too much remember you are not a LOLITA, you are a LOLA and you can go home, after ostentatiously giving away your tickets.

Enjoy!

SEE YOU AROUND.

APRÈS LE FRINGE

Having taken this advice, you will have survived the Fringe and had your money's worth – with luck even more than you expected or bargained for. Let us share experiences and admit to anxieties, mistakes, perks, deviousness and at times harmless competitive aggression. After the initial forays, one became immune to curious usually pitying glances quickly acquiring a to-the-manor-born sophistication while enjoying the frisson of excitement.

Don't you agree there was a nostalgia in seeing mini-clad-all-over youngsters snogging (is that word still fashionable?) and I am sure you are by now an authority on belly-button jewellery. Staring in queues was permissible. You must be glad you took a torch especially for The Pleasance and glad you had dispensed with cumbersome demanding friends. Finding a seat for one was so much easier and I hope you were luckier than me regarding the sex scenes. I didn't get enough this year, and not a peep at full frontal. However, I had lots of infidelity, ravishing, mental illness, sexual deviance and death and divorce so I was satisfied in some ways.

Although intrusive it was a thrill to help and advise overseas visitors and it'll be even more thrilling to accept their invitations to Toronto, Warsaw and definitely Wyoming.

Now on a less happy note, you are probably suffering from F.W.S. (Fringe Withdrawal Symptoms). The signs vary. You may find yourself joining a queue, any queue to anything or anywhere, or approaching a complete stranger and asking for a flyer or snatching his newspaper. I've just told one gentleman how much I enjoyed him last week! In fact, F.W.S. is not unlike jet lag. You might fall asleep suddenly or wake up unexpectedly and march into an empty home or walk up and down a church aisle. Do not worry about mild hallucinations – they are usually transient – as are unaccustomed "explicit" dreams, unfortunately.

It is unusual to have muscle twitches or pain as such, and miraculously your bladder will have improved (research needed here surely).

There is no definitive cure for Fringe Withdrawal Symptoms. I can only share my own experiences with you and advise:

- Television is no substitute.
- Drink heavily in the first week or avoid alcohol altogether.
- Don't take tablets of any kind – not even vitamins or placebos.
- Avoid daylight. Sleep in a darkened room for 2, preferably 3 days after your last show.
- Don't look at your Credit Card statements. Instead, think of all the money you saved by not going to the Festival "proper".
- After a few days, take a City Tour and go round and round all day reliving the venues as you pass. This is a type of mourning – think of it as a funeral procession.

The symptoms do get better, I promise, and it's not long to wait before the next Fringe programme arrives, detailed study of which effects a complete cure.

Recovery is accelerated by indulging in an alternative activity ASAP. Decide to indulge in that dubious something you've always wanted to do, especially if it can be done alone (or *á deux* or *á trois*) and incognito. Keep going.

CULTURE Rules OK.

"FOR ME"

Why do so many people ask us to do things for them? Even when we are consulting and paying.

The supermarket check-out girl says "Sign this for me".

The shampoo girl says "Sit here for me. Head back for me". Mercifully the stylist does not say "Cut your hair for me" or "Hold the scissors for me".

Bank clerks say "Check the money for me".

The dentist says "Rinse for me. Bite for me. Be relaxed for me".

The eye specialist says "Look up for me, look right for me, straight ahead for me. Eyes down for me. Blink for me". LOLA, after three consultations you are so in love with his voice so near to you as he looks into your eyes, that you would do anything for him. Maybe one day he'll say "Wink for me" or why not "Kiss for me".

Buying shoes you are told "Try this one on for me". Then "Try the other one on for me".

The doctor is much the same. "Say 'aah' for me. Breathe in for me. Hold it for me. Cough for me. Breathe out for me. Step on the scales for me. Take these tablets for me". Receptionists say "Sit over there for me". "Go and give a specimen for me".

Waiters say "Queue here for me. Take a seat for me. This table for me".

The masseur says "Roll over for me. Leg up for me. Bend over for me". And at the end, "Now have a drink of water for me". Having a facial it's "Smile for me. Pout for me. Close your eyes for me and frown for me".

It's the "FOR ME" syndrome, a 'me' fixation to make us beholden. "Open your mouth please" is OK but "Open your mouth for me" is control and threatening. It's a hierarchy. Yet when someone wants you to actually do something for them they leave out the 'for me' bit. Instead:- "Could you lend me a fiver?" "It's your turn to pay". "Babysitting would be useful". "Take these books back to the library as you're going". "You could get the tickets" – not a FOR ME to be heard.

At McDonald's they don't say "Eat this hamburger for me". Is that the secret of their success – no bullying?

It happens more to us LOLAs probably because we've forgotten how to do anything for ourselves! LOLA we must get in first and say "Wash my hair for me; look into my eyes for me; take my pulse for me; read this for me; I'm checking this bill for me; I'm rinsing my mouth for me; I'm putting my clothes back on for me … in other words STEAL the "For Me" control. Why not LOSE CONTROL and TAKE CONTROL saying "Not for you my darling. After all I'm paying".

Concerned relatives and friends are particularly difficult to deal with when they implore:- "Now don't rush for me; don't fall over for me". "Stand up for me". "Look smart for me". "Wear a coat for me". "And do try and remember for me" and "Try and be sensible for me" – as if, dear LOLA, your wish is to fracture your femur, freeze to death, or prefer to remember nothing – all en route to dementia.

Don't encourage such caring friends. Say nothing or turn the tables and tell them what to do for you. You will then be labelled "Difficult and demanding and rather ungrateful, but with all your wits about you". So have the TV and radio at full blast simultaneously and complain that they're always asking you to do something for them. LOLA, practise all this now before you get admitted to the nursing home where FOR ME is built into every request – or should I say 'instruction'.

In that case, it's simple. Just do the opposite – for them of course!

Equally patronising to a LOLA is the colleague who in discussion with you says "I can see where you're coming from" (little does she know) or "Let's not go there", as if you're offering to accompany her instead of just commenting on microwaves or drug addicts.

We LOLAs don't like it when complete strangers who we hope never to meet again say "See you later". It's tempting to say you sincerely hope not. But please don't. You'll give pedantic LOLAs a bad name. "See you later" does not have the same element of choice as "Have a nice day", which is comforting after a 'sunny-side up' breakfast. And without the 'For Me' it leaves you free to have as miserable a day as you like.

LOLA, you have the right to go anywhere, sit anywhere, open or close your mouth when you like, put your clothes on, or indeed take them off at any time – just for you.

Why not be difficult, ungrateful, independent and selfish. It's fun.

MARKET RESEARCH: LOLAS NOT REQUIRED

There have always been people with clipboards on our High Streets. Sometimes in isolation and sometimes in little groups. When they wear bright advertising clothes or have bright advertising umbrellas they appear as a kind of RASH. For example, in Princes Street there's a "wheal" of them at either end and a "pustule" outside The Overseas Club and another at The Old Waverley. It is all part of Market Research. The clipboard outbreak has never really been out of fashion, but is sometimes in abeyance – having another incubation period, but always returning with renewed vigour.

When challenged by a clipboard, most pedestrians walk hurriedly past – head down and an air of preoccupation, often fumbling for the mobile. I, however, slow my pace, hover, even dawdle, even stop, but they do not like me and do not want me. The reason is AGE. It is not paranoia. When I ask "why don't you interview me?" I'm told I fall into the too-old category. Even if I beg saying "I'm free, I'm free, I'll co-operate" I am rejected. They have been given their instructions – no old people and certainly no LOLAS (little old ladies alone).

This is Ageist. Ageism. Do we not still consume things after the age of 60? If you prick us do we not bleed? Are we not still consumers with the added advantage of experience in trial and error? We know all about Daz and Persil and Bold and countless others and are experts regarding top-loading or front-loading machines and spin cycles. We have opinions on every conceivable medicine for every conceivable organ of the body – and strategies for non-conceiving! We watch all the soaps and because of insomnia we are forced to watch late-night sex programmes and listen to Radio 5. We know what to do with parmesan, thongs, wasp-bites and halitosis and can advise on rent rebates, libraries, social workers, cholesterol, deep-vein thrombosis, pain control, winter fuel and Mr Kipling. We have time to have opinions on everything.

When one clipboarder told me "not you madam, I'm researching champagne" I smiled and replied, "What a pity, I only bath in it". So, of course, I had to celebrate my quick thinking with a glass or three of MOET.

Oh, for the good old days of being asked if we prefer margarine or butter, and the tasting thereof, or the knock on the door, the ring of the bell to be presented with a box of paper tissues or a box of Cadbury's Roses. What's more you didn't need make-up or a posh hair-do – they liked you dishevelled, preferably in short nightie and slippers – like Cherie. However, if you are on the street and it is snowing, do not be too excited. Refuse to answer questions on the pavement or in a doorway. Insist on taking the lift (you are a LOLA) to the room base in the Hotel, and expect a cuppa and a biscuit, and while you're there, get warmed up and use the toilet.

You are presented with a choice of pictures or a questionnaire which is a work of art, designed to confuse an intelligent LOLA. I suggest the following guidelines:

1. Always answer "NO" or "DON'T KNOW".
2. Tick the box saying you never use the product (preferably indicate you've never heard of it) and mention a rival product which you swear by.
3. On a scale of marks from 0–5, say 5, especially if you've never used the products.
4. Complain that it's tiring and hard work – perhaps another cup of coffee...
5. Point out any spelling mistakes – there always are.
6. Half-way through it's fun to ask the Researcher for her Authority Badge or her C.V. and show a great

interest in her education and her husband or children as well as asking casually if she's had a police check. You can't be too careful tell her, I'm sure she'll understand.

All in all it could prove to be a worthwhile two hours.

Sadly, not every LOLA will be lucky enough to be accosted when out and about, and it is frustrating to see even elderly men being approached. Do not give up, concentrate instead on the questionnaires that arrive in the post – usually with a free pen – entreating you to complete, and of course reply to those questionnaires that fall out of magazines. Do not be tempted to throw them in the bin. Settle down to answer. A 50/50 truthful and untruthful ratio is OK. Don't leave a box unticked – it arouses suspicion. And don't waste your time on anything less than 4 pages – you will be amazed how therapeutic it can be.

The whole exercise is better than counselling or aromatherapy and cheaper than a "Psychoanalysis" session. After 4 or 5 pages you will have revealed everything about your home, your job, relationships, finances, dress and colour preferences, car, holiday haunts, response to adultery, drugs and drinking habits and aspects of your husband you'd never previously considered. Your past and present will have been highlighted.

The future is then up to you. You can decide to move house, change your nail varnish, learn Gaelic, order oysters, go on Trisha, sleep in the library or discard the *Mail on Sunday*, your cousin/best friend or your husband.

Believe me, you will be a different woman, maybe not even be a LOLA anymore – just a LOLL (little old lady laughing or even little old lady with lover).

THE AUTHORITIES

I cite my occupation as housewife and carer because I have a house, I am a wife and I care for a mother-in-law who suffers from dementia and I am the designated carer (that is I get paid) of my son Kenneth who is age 14 and has severe learning difficulties.

I manage OK because I am fit and healthy and they say I am "of a happy disposition" and I am lucky enough to go to the bingo every Tuesday night and I have to admit, every now and again, I have a "girls" night out and too much to drink – vodka!!

That lovely Margaret Thatcher let us buy our Council house, so we've no mortgage, but money is tight. Trevor, my husband, is a porter and no longer gets overtime but he helps on weekends etc. with a removals firm to make extra when he can. He's a good husband. His mother, my mother-in-law, who lives with us doesn't really know Trevor anymore and she's always getting me mixed up with her mother or her aunty or the lady in the shop. I've got used to her now. She doesn't mean no harm when she smashes things or pushes me against the wall. It's because she's frustrated, bless her. She gets taken to the club on Mondays and Thursdays with outings in the Summer every month so I manage to work on the shelves in the supermarket on those days. Oh, and she gets invited to two parties at Christmas time.

And I've got Kenny. My Kenny is my baby boy. Not so much a baby now – nearly 5"10" and only 14 and plenty of beef on him. He goes to a special school and the helpers on the bus just love him.

Everybody's quite nice but I do have problems with the Authorities. I keep getting letters out of the blue asking peculiar things. It must be the computer coming up with my name. It's always me who gets the letters – never Trevor. Maybe 'cause I sign myself "guardian" always.

Sometimes the letters are a bit funny. I got one saying my fence would be repaired last Tuesday so I phoned back to say I was working and I didn't have a fence, it's a wall round the back garden. I laughed.

I didn't laugh when I got a letter after Easter asking where Kenny would be going after leaving school, after "O" Levels. I had to tick a box to say: Stay on for Highers, College or university, or work. I made an extra box saying "other". It upset me really. Another letter from the Research Department asked me and my husband to go for a blood test, something to do with passing on a disease – something genetics. Trevor said they could p*** off. I'm 52 and had the change. I didn't write back. I'll say I didn't get the letter if they ask. I hope Kenneth's not my fault, I mean being as he is. I never thought about it until that letter came because he was a difficult birth – over 2 days in labour, and I thought it was that.

The man from the Attendance Allowance is a regular. It's got a different name now. It's never the same person but most of them just make a quick visit, in and out – "any change Mrs Gordon?" "No." "Fine." They sometimes don't wait for a cup of tea, just pick up a couple of chocolate biscuits and run.

But oh dear! the Mobility man – nasty! Always trying to trip me up. Last time he told Kenneth to step out of the back door into the garden and he watched from the kitchen window. "There, he can walk," he said. But there were no steps. He can't walk to the bus stop. I have to hold him and help him everywhere. He should have a wheelchair. He told me Kenneth might qualify next time as he may have deteriorated.

But I must be fair, I did get a lovely letter from the Deputy Assistant Director about me wanting a commode for my mother-in-law. He was glad to hear from me and said it would be on the agenda for the next meeting in April. That's not long really, only four months. I've written to say I appreciate he is a very busy man, and thank him for taking such a personal interest in my commode.

Another person who's lovely is my doctor but you need to be ill for him to come and Kenny stays pretty healthy considering.

I do not have a soft spot for the social workers. They talk differently, most of them argue with everything I say. I think it's because they don't understand and haven't seen Kenny. I wish they'd come when he's not at school. The nice ones don't argue. They are the opposite. They agree with me and write down everything I say and want me to have a shower and a ramp and a dryer in the house. The last social worker said she was horrified that I hadn't had a holiday in 3 years and she wanted to arrange respite care but I don't want that, Kenny calls it SPITE CARE. Funny how the dates are never the same times as the Home can take mother-in-law. Just my luck. Anyway, I needn't bother, that social worker's left now. I've cottoned on now that they give Kenny to the young ones in training and they only stay six weeks.

I was crying after the last one. Then I got cross and had a brainwave. I phoned up the N.S.P.C.C. anonymous-like, I said Mrs Gordon was neglecting her boy Kenneth. I'd seen bruises and lots of shouting and him out in the garden without a coat. Two of them came round that day. The house was a tip and I had a bottle of wine on the kitchen units. I think they made a note that I'm a drinker (me! I fall asleep after one bacardi and coke!). They come over regular now and go over the whole house. I've got a downstairs toilet and shower and a fireguard and two extra phones. I ask for something every time. I don't even stay in for them because I know they'll be back to check on me. I always mention my bingo and talk about the pub.

The school psychologist I hate. She drags me to meetings and they are always late starting because we have to wait for about ten people to come. They all read out reports and tell me what they recommend for Kenny – a college place, but there's no place. I'll worry about that later. I'll have to give up my supermarket days.

So you see, my Kenny's not the problem, it's the authorities, but I'm lucky really to have a good husband and blessed really to have Kenny.

I just hope this lump I found yesterday is nothing serious, just worry I expect.

I'll ask Janice at the bingo tonight.

REALITY INTERVIEWING

There is little that takes place now which does not warrant an Interview of some kind. We listen on the radio to first-hand comments from bystanders, witnesses, experts, celebrities, relatives or friends. We watch every detail on TV and "Read all about it" in the newspapers.

There is now a predictability about reportage. How I long for someone somewhere in some context (serious or comic) to give honest from the heart replies – Reality Replies.

Many scenarios come to mind.

SENIOR POLITICIAN

A classical interview following a tragedy of some kind.

What are your views and comments about the circumstances and impact of this dreadful event?

Good Afternoon,

Let me first of all say that my first thoughts are with the relatives. Let me take this opportunity to indicate my personal sympathy to the families of loved ones. I can't imagine what they're going through.

Yes it is a tragedy. It is too early to speculate. Details are being diligently investigated and I have instigated an Enquiry which will report directly to me and through me to the Government.

There have been Enquiries before and nothing has changed. It is puzzling isn't it?

A lot has changed but there are still lessons to be learned. The public are rightly concerned and all Political Parties are united in this.

Could this have been avoided? How does it appear to you?

It is of course easy to be wise after the event. It has not been our finest hour. We must leave no stone unturned to get at the reasons behind this. It may be mechanical error, or something more personal.

What persons do you mean?

We must get on top of it.

Do you think this accident could be the result of poor investment on the part of the Government?

I do not want to pre-empt the Enquiry. I have every confidence in Lord Kant who is the leading light on investigations like this and I have every faith in the British judicial system, which is fair and thorough – not like that of other countries.

When will we know the result of the Enquiry?

I have asked for it to start immediately, but these things take time. It should be available by the end of the year.

That is 8 months or more.

It takes time to unravel the many components which may have resulted in this sad event. We must be diligent and must not get it wrong and above all we must make sure nothing like this ever happens again.

Have you any other thoughts?

I must say there has been a media frenzy over this. It has been blown up out of all proportion by the media, by TV and the press, even in your own paper and on your programme.

We must keep a perspective on this and I repeat I have every confidence we will get answers.

I have every faith in Lord Kant who is a most eminent expert in this and I cannot prejudice his enquiry by commenting further. But we will take note of his findings and I am absolutely determined nothing like this will ever happen again.

Thank you.

It's been a pleasure.

MATURITY – AT LAST

One expects some physical deterioration with advancing age – high blood pressure, arthritis, the odd fracture and dizzy turn, *sans* this and *sans* that until you reach *sans* everything. Why not develop a mindset to expect the good bits – bus pass, memories, concessions, no pretending and free prescriptions.

And with luck it will be *avec* everything in working order.

There may be slight intellectual back-tracking but emotionally and character-wise you have never been better equipped. It's called MATURITY. As a LOLA you have it at last.

It's the creeping up of subtle indignities that take you by surprise. But remember there is a PRO and a CON to everything.

Signs and symptoms of maturity vary. Some examples…

- Before bed time your list of "Things to do tomorrow" becomes progressively shorter, along with the feeling "what does it matter". You can use the same list the following day or the following week.
- You graciously accept the seat, even if offered by someone older than you.
- The TV can be cruel. You don't know the person "whose house it is" and you've never heard of the celebrity victim on *This is Your Life* and would never "get them out of there" or even want to.

   On the other hand you can sit cosily with great-grandpa and teenagers watching "Explicits". No problem. It shows you are well adjusted and knowledgeable. Explain what is going on and the correct name for it, or ask the youngsters to explain.

And you have a choice – say you never did that, or you always did that, years ago. Such responses indicate one's security. It's called "Savoir Faire". Switching off the TV or leaving the room means you haven't got it.

- In restaurants you ask the waiter for a doggie bag and take the ½ steak you've left home.
- Lavatories are no longer a problem. Announce you're desperate and jump the queue. In France or Italy the confident LOLA goes to the MEN'S.
- No more inhibitions. You can leave a dinner party anytime – even after the paté, and refuse a lift home. Fear of "familiarity" is not the worry – it's having to wait until 2am before he is ready to leave.

  Indeed your behaviour at buffet parties and receptions is an excellent indicator of maturity. Sit near the food but nearer to the drinks. Sample everything. Discard the crusts on sandwiches and pop them in a bin – or why not in someone else's pocket. Drop the gold wrapper of a Ferrero Rocher on the floor (what do they do with them at the Ambassador's Reception?). Hide the 4 drumstick bones on your plate, on plates of others or just gift them back to the waiter. Getting 2nd or 3rd helpings requires skill, especially with wine. Best to find a new empty glass and just say "When do I have some wine?" This manoeuvre can be repeated, or say to a total stranger "Be a darling and get me some liquid – preferably wine."

- A really mature person does not apologise, does not explain but is critical. The fault lies elsewhere.

- When photographs are taken, you confidently position yourself centre front; especially at weddings. It's fantastic if you can catch the bouquet!

- Being so old you can take the arm of a stranger at any time.

- The mature LOLA talks comfortably about everything – about ailments of a personal nature, about divorce and adulteries, difficult relatives, and even talks about MONEY. Give nothing away. Let them speculate whether you are watching the pennies (complain of the price of porridge) or rolling in money (give details of the Dow Jones and the Stock market).

- You can ignore "young" menopausal friends who exhort you to take up orienteering, darts or research into Chinese dialects, and say life is just beginning. It's not and you're "endopausal" and can stop achieving. They are ridiculous. In fact a complete disregard for one's effect on others is mandatory and conclusive evidence of Maturity. You are allowed to be contradictory and outrageous.

LOLA, you are now mature. Exaggerate your past. You are already pigeon-holed and labelled so be abandoned, care not a fig and enjoy.

I find it remarkably satisfying to confess to sins you wish you had committed. However, LOLA, there's still time.

WORDS IN FASHION

It is not easy to understand why some words are destined to become popular, used excessively, have several meanings and loved by everyone. Basically they have become fashionable.

Basically let me start with:

BASICALLY – universally popular. The All-Time favourite. Used sometimes several times in one sentence and always to begin any answer, therefore beloved by interviewees. It is used as an adverb, adjective or adjectival noun (remember those) and is particularly effective when used on its own – in isolation, just dropped into the conversation, unrelated to anything gone before or indeed anything which follows – except maybe just with a smile, there can be a poignancy about its nakedness.

It has basically stood the test of time, and basically will always be with us … basically.

ROBUST – This became a sudden and surprising front runner with many uses e.g. The athlete is in Robust health and gave a Robust tackle in Robust clothing on a Robust pitch in a Robust manner but he is less Robust now.

There was a definite decline in its usage but it has returned to fashion mainly thanks to politicians who study matters Robustly and give a Robust response after a Robust investigation; and maintain a Robust defence in reply to the Robust challenge of the Robust questioning of the Robust opposition. Curiously he or she is not always in Robust physical condition but needs to have a Robust attitude with Robust opinion or able to use the word to robustly camouflage obscure, erroneous or confusing information.

Robust is also gaining ground at the BBC.

SOME – has to be mentioned. Although simple and sometimes succinct it has some dozen usages, as one can illustrate:

Some 200 people arrived with some trepidation, some ten minutes ago, having walked some way amid some confusion but showing some respect. Some were disappointed and did some complaining about some of the music accompanying some of the entertainment. Some PARTY that!!

ACTUALLY – is an Also-Ran but used a great deal by the upper classes.

ICON – a relative newcomer which has sneaked to centre stage at great speed. ICONS are everywhere.

One can VISIT ICONS such as The Taj Mahal, Mont St. Michel, the bulbous biomes of the Eden Project, John O'Groat's signpost, Harrods, a New York yellow cab, Tower Bridge, Glasgow's Squinty Bridge etc.

WEARING: in a waft of Elnett hairspray Jackie O's glasses, Rolex, Hermes scarf, an A Line, New Look or Mary Quant style dress and carrying the new Icons handbag.

ADMIRING: Madonna, Jordan's Iconic pair as well as Iconic monuments and the Dulux Dog, the Beatles Zebra Crossing, and LISTENING in the company of rugby, football and boxing icons and gazing at celebrities and hairdressers who have iconic jobs!

It is easy to overlook that Emotions are also described as ICONS, such as the Icon of Embarrassment, Muslim Culture, Picasso's response to war, the image of Myra Hindley's eyes, Iraq an Icon of defeat with Guatanemo suicides an Icon of injustice.

Tourist agencies anywhere could set up Icon Tours.

One could get on a red double-decker with a Clippie, passing black cabs and monuments listening to Shakespeare, Pavarotti, the bagpipes etc.

In Edinburgh the Tour could include a stop at Jenners for shortbread, whisky, cashmere and a sporran, all ICONS while gazing at that Castle Icon.

Followed by a look at the jagged sit-in Iconic windows of the Scottish Parliament before popping over to the Forth Bridges via Britannia. Icon Tours would be lucrative for any city. Some ICONS are soon to be built we are told.

You too can be an ICON of something – if not you are a nobody.

Already you wear/eat/read/smell/use, admire and circulate among Icons in a haze of Iconic emotions. Your day (and night) is awash with Icons, with more to come. LUCKY YOU.

To bring you up to date, there is a new word threatening to overtake all others. It is:

SUB-PRIME – imported from America (a multi-Icon country) and fast gathering popularity, excitement, even LOVE. It is a sort of Affliction/Disease or Illness? Research shows it can spread, even person-to-person. Some people have sub-prime personalities, but most men are resistant and may never have a sub-prime attack, whereas it is prevalent in women who often become addicted.

It has poisoned the Bank sector, hit the Mortgage Market and soon you may have to tick (✓) several sub-prime boxes before qualifying for government perks.

LOLA we have survived sub-prime – wages, holidays, wardrobe, bank account, handbag, in-laws, a sub-prime husband and sub-prime emotions. There is even a romanticism about the sub-prime condition. Cure involves recklessly indulging and denying yourself nothing. Aim for Prime or Super-Prime.

To summarise the WORD SUPREMACY CHART. There is SOME doubt ACTUALLY whether SUB-PRIME is ROBUST enough to overtake ICON, but BASICALLY surely reigns supreme.

… Basically.

BE YOUR OWN FINANCIAL ADVISER

LOLA you can't do a worse job of your finances than the dapper young man who has all the time to call, have tea and cakes and chat with you until you sign, then he's off. Women are proving good on the Stock Exchange and are overtaking men in the Riches stakes.

We come in all shapes and financial sizes. Let me compartmentalise, and you can chose which category best illustrates your position. Let's start from the top and deteriorate:

- Mega Rich – surprisingly nice people. These should give three quarters away. Ingratiate yourself LOLA.
- Rich – not so nice. Should give half away. LOLA don't cultivate them.
- Middle Of The Road – thee and me. Give nothing.
- On The Breadline – they hide it.
- Very Poor – don't hide it.
- In Debt – someone else does the worrying for you.

I have general advice for you all. Don't take too many risks. Spread your portfolio even if it only means a series of jam jars on the mantelpiece. At your age, investing for one or two years is prudent, five years is hopeful, ten years is foolhardy, and twenty years is dicing with death.

I do hope you've got your **Income Tax Returns** off in time. Don't pay an Accountant – you've had to find all the details anyway. Do it yourself – it's liberating. You'll know then how much or how little you've got. The first time you fill in the form, it's daunting and will take you three weeks night and day; next time three days and thereafter you'll do it in three hours.

Treat the form as a short story about you. It can be amusing but is mostly boring. However, the confusing bits are the double negatives like "Is your name and address on the front wrong?" Tick the box marked "Yes".

Don't ignore the 35 pages of Guidelines – make it bedtime reading. It cures insomnia. If you do not need the Supplementary forms for Property, Shares, Dependants, Disability, Overseas Banking, Self-Employed or a Student and No Lodger, you may get depressed and feel your life is not exciting enough. You'll cheer up when you itemise the gifts that you've given to charities. Has to be money. Old clothes don't count.

Complete it on April 30th and enjoy your summer holidays. Most people forget to sign it – not you.

When you get the bill an abbreviation to watch is <u>CR</u>. It means credit of course but not to you – it's to them and you owe it. A charming idiosyncrasy of the Tax Office.

LOLAs are already frugal. It's a legacy from the War, Coupons and Rationing. I suggest further savings. For newspapers go to the Library or Debenhams or a Four-Star Hotel. If you're in a corner out of sight you can tear out the bit you want, or take buses anywhere until you find the free Metro.

Charity Shops:

You know all about these. Don't do local. Go to a new area or preferably a new town where you won't meet your neighbours or your previous boss. Try on lots – Houdini-like – in the tiny dressing room. No need to buy.

Sample Food:

You can do away with breakfast. Saturday mornings are good on delicatessen counters. On a toothpick five cheeses, two each of ham/turkey are very filling – approximately 150 calories, washed down with three samples of wine another 50 calories. (Jenners is best for whisky – portions are thimble-full but the chat about Scottish islands is enlightening.)

Allowances:

Be sure to get them all and exploit. There's always something you deserve.

Pregnancy is not an option for you LOLA, and becoming a student at Open or 'closed' University is a gamble.

Senior Citizens Cinema Mornings are cheap. Go early and you can rejoin and rejoin the queue for coffee and biscuits.

If you are astute, special visiting days at Show Houses often involve a glass of wine and canapés. Dress well as if you intend to buy.

I hesitate to advise gate-crashing weddings but you are old enough to add gravitas to the respectful mourners at a funeral wake.

Become a model. Offer yourself as a guinea-pig at the hairdressers. You will emerge quite changed. If you are lucky enough to have a rare medical condition – hearing, smell or visual problems, funny nails, indeed any funny syndrome – you can allow yourself to be a body for medical student exams, with meals, taxis, escort and expenses. Dextro-cardia, (a heart on the wrong side) is a winner to fail the cocky applicants and you deserve extra expenses. Charge more. Make it a major earning opportunity. There are disadvantages, you may have to carry a receptacle to collect 24-hour urine specimen. No one wants your blood. You're too old and they assume you've led a too-eventful life.

LOLA please don't hand over your house/flat to a film crew. They alter windows, even walls and the neighbours will resent you. However, it's lucrative to take in at Festival time the entire "crew" of a provincial theatre group. You only need one spare room and mattresses (with unlimited milk and sliced bread as free luxury extras). Fleece them. They are young and will get over it. If necessary move out of your own room.

You will have noticed none of these opportunities are against the law. You are law abiding. Stay that way, unless of course you fancy a couple of weeks comfortable and well fed at Her Majesty's Pleasure. If so, the opportunities are limitless – shoplifting, soliciting, causing a disturbance, drunk and disorderly, GBH and wandering with intent. Then you can get a Legal Aid lawyer to make a lot of money for himself and free you.

LOLA I advise from experience and add to the quote: "I've been rich, I've been poor – rich is better". But poor can bring a lot of fun.

Modestly I'm planning to become an Independent Financial Advisor for LOLAs. Payment by instalments will not be appreciated, because one's never sure of the time-span allotted. Watch this space!

Applications welcomed for position of Agony Aunt to work exclusively with and with a bias towards, Little Old Ladies Alone (LOLAs).

No one has experienced and weathered the vicissitude of life more than a LOLA. Such extensive knowledge of the slings and arrows (both Cupid's and deadly) should not be wasted. A LOLA will have survived:- unemployment, drudgery, discrimination, marriage, being dumped, divorce, pregnancies, adultery, the high life, addictions of varying kinds, riches, poverty, the menopause and now the endopause.

Let others benefit from your extensive knowledge.

Advice to applicants:-

> Do not pontificate.
> Get straight to the point.
> Keep it short – long-winded replies are counter-productive.
> Avoid swearing but using F*** or b***** or b******
> is permissible.
> Care not about insulting the inadequate who's written –
> especially if a man.

Some succinct examples to illustrate:-

> Question: No one's interested in my views on anything.
> Answer: So shut up!

> Question: I keep remembering my night of abandonment in
>   Belfast.
> Answer: Go there again.

Question: My daughter-in-law is vegetarian. What about Christmas?

Answer: Super. Save money. Serve vegetable stew, then splash out on vino/vodka/vermouth/vine leaves and vegetarian Christmas Crackers. They could contain sachets of cumin, garlic cloves, strong chillies, or pistachios.

Question: I've been caught shop-lifting from Ann Summers.

Answer: Get your husband to confess he forced you into it.

Question: There's scaffolding and workers all round my house. I like walking around in the nude.

Answer: Keep going. They've seen it all before but tell your visitors to come fully clothed.

Question: The vicar's wife has a fancy man. Should I spill the beans?

Answer: Most certainly. Let it slip out at the Church Fete.

Question: My mixer doesn't work.

Answer: Read the instructions or press the switch down darling.

Question: My grandson says he's "come-out" and is gay.

Answer: Be delighted. Tell him to wear a warm coat and have a party where he'll meet a nice girl, who, like him, is not depressed.

Question: My elderly neighbour wants me to go swinging.

Answer: Don't be tempted. Suggest LINE or POLE dancing instead.

Question: My cerise outfit for my granddaughter's wedding clashes with the ridiculous red of the other grandmother.

Answer: (a) Tell her to buy a more suitable colour.

(b) Don't go.

(c) Clash.

Question: I am addicted to alcohol and stealing. Which is
worse?
Answer: Only steal when you're sober and drink afterwards.

Question: I've waited a year for a hearing aid.
Answer: Move to Stuttgart.

Question: My friends refuse to push me in my wheelchair.
Answer: Go electric, drive at speed and frighten them to
death.

Question: I'm worried about inheritance tax.
Answer: My private telephone number is in the post. You
have a lovely house.

For those who find this type of advice too challenging and
can't cope with confrontation, you can explore other
conventional avenues.

- Your GP – he/she can't give much counselling in his
  allotted 4 minutes, but will refer you to a specialist –
  only a two-year wait.
- The gamut of "Alternatives": massage,
  aromatherapy, stones, homeopathy, herbs, the gym
  and Tai Chi and Floating – try them all.
- Victim Support – most LOLAs qualify as victims of
  something or other.
- Group Therapy – Alcoholics Anonymous, Women's
  Institute, Weightwatchers, Keep Fit and the pub.
  Wonderful – and you'll meet other fat gambling
  alcoholics.
- NOT the dentist – discussion is one way.
- Other counsellors to choose from are:
  Your vicar – but often too young and
  inexperienced for you.
  Traffic Wardens – their Assertiveness
  Training will help you.
  The trusted hairdresser – who has learned on
  the job and will agree with your predicament.

So you will see there are extensive Support Systems available. Help is everywhere, so how can you avoid being happy. However, the Agony Aunt is trusted and has proved itself over years. Besides you can sign your letter incognito "A Smith (Ms) Morningside".

Application please with C.V. and References. These will not be followed up but a police check will be scrutinised as we know personality disorders do not diminish with age although mercifully physical prowess does. Send photograph – not too glamorous and no cleavage.

This is a very competitive position. You owe it to help fill the world with happy and well-adjusted and resigned old people. HURRY.

Interview

GAME SHOW

Well now – let's look at the score Helen my darling.
You've not managed to score but you're still lucky. You'll
have our special embossed address book. Have you enjoyed
yourself?

No.
It's been terrible.

Right. Well – Oh dear! Tears! And you still look beautiful
even when you're crying.

Perhaps someone will take Helen away.

COLUMNISTS – ARE THEY CLONES?

It seems to me that almost all the newspaper publications: magazines – cheap and sophisticated; dailies and weeklies – tabloid and broadsheet – as well as those specialising on travel, hobbies, crafts, the occult and all aspects of science – all have "regular" columnists. (I'm not sure about pornography – are there regular columnists? I'm not an expert. Not yet!)

The regulars are mostly female, and there is always a fetching photograph at the top corner of the article.

I have to say the writings are usually clever, topical and amusing – at first. However, after several hundred issues there is little left about the writer, her husband or his wife, their children, the neighbours, in-laws, parents, teachers, ex-boyfriends, workmen or others in their orbit that is exciting to the regular reader.

Why do these relatives or "friends" not object to their idiosyncrasies being aired in print? The children are surely mortified to have their habits described in detail, and the husband surely not pleased to be "exposed" to work colleagues, especially when conversations are written verbatim. No topic is sacred. Why does no one sue?

Shopping, holidays, kitchen disasters, garden disasters, bowel habits, unwanted presents, nits, public speaking, lost socks, flooded kitchens and family possessions appear and re-appear in the column whereas it would be inconceivable to miss out on:- Easter, Guy Fawkes, Mothers Day (or Fathers and Grandparents), Valentines, Sports Days, Pancake Day, the Equinox (who cares?) and Xmas! Xmas! Xmas!

And every now and again – to keep us informed, there are personal titbits about "Y" fronts, sexual prowess and the merits of thongs, birthing pools, alcohol and faking it. We wait with bated breath in anticipation of adultery, romps and divorce.

And suddenly we no longer care. Reality writing become boring. So we try another columnist and another opera.

At age 76¾ I will write a column. It will be refreshingly different – full of excellent advice and observations and entirely biased.

It will be embarrassing to family and acquaintances. Besides, the persons quoted being old or older will not care, will not sue, will not recognise themselves and might likely be dead.

So envy, slander, flattery and bitchiness will be allowed and non-attributable, but there will always be stories of love and passion and sex. Old age ensures more memories – and more vanity. It will be my confessional, and reminiscence therapy.

(Children's Story)

BIG TED

When I was age 2 we left our nice home in London to come to live in Scotland. It was me and my sister, age 3, and my baby brother with my mum and daddy.

I wasn't sure about Scotland and I was frightened but I had "Big Ted" with me and my sister had her doll. My baby brother just had mum.

I didn't cry at the airport, not even with all the noise and I went up the steps to the aeroplane very carefully, holding on to the sides. When the aeroplane went up into the sky I closed my eyes and I closed my ears. Then something terrible happened when I opened my eyes:

I could not find Big Ted, I had lost him, I had dropped him on the steps, I had left him in London, I would not see him again, and he would not see me again.

Then I did cry and cry and cry. The lady gave me orange juice and a minty chocolate but I still cried.

Then, you'll never guess – the pilot started speaking on the aeroplane radio. He said: "We are flying very high in the sky and if you look out of the window you will see Manchester Town."

Then he said:

"I am lucky to have someone to help me fly the plane and be nice company for me. I have a teddy here with me – quite a big teddy but he got lost and had to walk up the aeroplane steps on his own so he's having a rest in the seat next to me. Is there a girl sitting near the back who has lost a teddy bear?

Please come to the front – to me the pilot and you can see if you know him. He says he's going to live in Scotland."

I was crying all the way to the pilot's office. And there next to the pilot and all strapped in WAS MY BIG TED.

On the way back to my seat, I was not crying and everyone clapped. But I didn't say anything, I didn't look at anybody, I didn't eat my chocolate, I didn't look out of the window, I just hugged my Big Ted all the time – I never closed my eyes.

The new house was big with lots of rooms and doors. It was a bit cold with a coldy smell. My sister let me have the bed in the corner and there was plenty of room for me and Big Ted and my hot water bottle.

I didn't tell any of my new friends about the aeroplane and I didn't tell them my nappy was wet. I just said we'd had an adventure and Big Ted was very brave on the plane and I was quite brave.

You must remember to be very careful when you walk up the steps to an aeroplane. You might lose your special friend.

HOSPITAL VISITING

A LOLA is inevitably expected to, indeed feels obliged to, spend much time on the popular "hobby" of "Hospital Visiting", so it is wise to have a management plan. Allow approximately four hours per visit (anything up to eight hours for a good funeral).

It's best to phone in advance to announce you will be visiting. Arrive ten minutes into the visiting hours, when the stampede is over and you can make an entrance.

Please wear something unusual and flamboyant. A largish hat or boa is ideal. It gives the ward something to talk about when you've gone – you are just being kind really.

You will of course have brought a present. Please no grapes, no chocolates, no air freshener and a tiny pot plant is more classy than flowers. If you have to bring flowers and can't find a vase, throw somebody else's expensive arrangement out and use that vase.

A word of warning against recklessly buying magazines at the last minute. Sick elderly patients do not and should not want to (and it's not good for them) read about: bungee-jumping, the *Which* report on thongs, making your own wine, fifty things to do before you're thirty, my husband was a woman, or how to fake it – a LOLA already knows. Equally insensitive are leaflets on stair-lifts or "How to write a Will". However, coins for the telephone, stamps and alcohol are always welcome.

In the ward deciding where to sit is important. On the bed, on the locker or, if necessary, steal a chair from another bed.

CONVERSATION is the most stressful and boring part. You must not be too doom-laden or too flippant. It is easy to offend. These suggestions will help:-

- Complain about the long journey to get there, and how you forgot your bus pass.
- Concentrate at once on her illnesses. There'll be more than three, and by good luck you will have had them all, as well as all the investigations, so you can give expert personal and graphic advice.
- On a lighter note stress that she must spoil herself with wine and a toddy at night and concentrate on meditating. Tell her she can refuse physiotherapy. It's painful and sometimes crippling. In fact she could refuse everything, and become "difficult" – the ward "character".
- Update on all the weddings and funerals she's missed, and describe everyone's clothes, noting that her sister-in-law wore the same floral outfit as before. It's done two weddings and two funerals to your knowledge.
- Find a suitable moment to ask if they've given her a Pace Maker. Someone should know before the cremation.
- Ask about other visitors, especially the ones who haven't come (because of the parking problem). Express surprise about them all.
- Comment on the cleanliness or otherwise of the ward, and say your cousin went in with nothing – she's a hypochondriac – and came out with MRSA.

It's thoughtful to bring a camera and take her photograph showing the drip and the tubes. It will be a nice reminder, and a talking point later with neighbours.

When conversation flags go off and visit ALL the other patients, conscious or less so. Think of it as a ward round and forget no one, especially if it's a popular mixed ward. At some beds whisper a lot.

Stay a long time at least until the tea trolley comes round. It's OK to chat with the WRVS lady and accept tea and a cake, but do go out on the balcony if you need to smoke.

Don't fall asleep, but you could have a "sort of funny turn". Someone will then surely offer you a lift home – but you must recover enough to wave and shout "Cheerio" to everybody.

You will be exhausted, but know that you've brought such happiness to so many poor sick old people.

DECLUTTERING

Decluttering is fashionable now, as revealed in topics such as "Find Yourself Amid The Chaos" and "The Life Laundry" as well as numerous storage ideas in the magazines.

LOLA you may not have a garage or attic full of valuable junk, so a car boot sale on Sunday is not appropriate; but you have a house full of clothes not worn and never will be worn, books you'll never read or never re-read, make-up galore not to mention the twenty-one bottles of perfume bought by relatives on flights home from package holidays. (Equivalent to 7 relatives, 3 holidays). You have enough L'Air du Temps to outlast you. China and unwanted gifts remain in their boxes, and the mantelpiece is full of ornaments, indicating a rich and varied life, but nevertheless clutter. Get rid at last of the blue jars accumulated since you inadvertently said in 1990 that you liked Stilton. You now have fourteen – minus the two eaten.

It's best to get a ruthless friend, a critical acquaintance or a curious neighbour to help with the job of decluttering. Close your eyes as she organises bin-bags, one for charity, another for the items which frankly are not good enough for charity, and a bag of things for auction. She designates a small carrier bag for "to keep" and another for herself. She will blitz your food shelves. Ten-year-old mincemeat, marmalade and Mulligatawny soup goes straight into the bin. No questions asked.

But you'll have to tolerate remarks such as "I never liked you in this dress", "Purple is not your colour, even now you're old". "This jug is cracked" "What's this for?" 1989 means the eye drops are well past the sell-by date. This clock/heater/radio doesn't work, and the dried flowers are too dried. Do you need three kettles and this road map doesn't show any motorways.

What about that piano stool? It needs to be upholstered. Get rid of it but first take out grandma's Piano Exercises and Hymns and keep them for another few years. Besides it's thirty years since you had a piano.

Get your helper or someone to take the stuff away pronto. If it's left you'll unpack it all, having changed your mind. You don't have to be friendly with her ever again. The motto is "if in doubt throw it out." If you have anything big like a fridge or bed, you have a dilemma. Consider the future environment for your grandchildren, and ask the council to dispose of it. No problem they say, but you have to carry the aforementioned fridge or bed single-handed LOLA and get it to the pavement before 7am – the night before is not allowed, and you need to make an appointment for this a week ahead.

After this Exodus you now have the space and are ready to receive Christmas gifts – more clutter but a different breed of clutter.

Golden rule is to keep gifts for a year, then give away. Label clearly so that cousin Flo doesn't receive her present back next year. Return unwanted gifts, but you need the receipt. Don't feel obliged to get something similar in a different colour or different size. Get something totally new. When taking things back join a long queue. The shop assistant will be too harassed to question you. Be tactful but if you feel like being tactless say things like "This jumper's a monstrosity, I don't like it. You shouldn't have sold it to my friend". After all you can be crotchety and tactless. It's a perk of being old. Tell your relatives graphically and exaggerate about your contretemps in the shop. They will dine out on the hilarious account of your atrocious and rude behaviour. But you're a LOLA. How droll!

A present from any male must be kept, and if not worn as an outer or under garment then put it on the mantelpiece. This prompts conversation and you can show off.

So now with all this room and space, off to the Sales. LOLA resist queuing in your sleeping bag with soup. It's foolhardy and you'll always be pushed or elbowed into being the last into the shop. A new cushion or cardigan, even with pockets, is not worth it.

Go instead three weeks later. Prices are rockbottom. They need the floor space (£50 has become £25, then £10.00, then £5). There are no crowds and few decisions and you will find what you've always wanted.

You will be able to celebrate your tidy uncluttered house, indeed your house is now almost empty. No more gazing at the ugly stuff you had, and there's a box of presents waiting to be given to friends next Christmas. You will feel rather naked (remember that?) but freed of clutter.

LOLA to be serious, it'll be less work for next of kin and neighbours when you pass away and less snooping, with fewer derogative remarks about your habits. You can rest happy.

WORKMEN

When it becomes necessary to have workmen in one's house, a LOLA is at their mercy. One can do little to get a promise of morning or afternoon, so you have to be up and respectable by 7.30 a.m. Then you just wait. I suspect the average waiting time is nine and a half hours, anything up to one and a half days – as well as four telephone calls.

I am petitioning the Local Authority to introduce classes, day and evening on the subject of how to cope. No two visiting workmen are the same, every one with his individual idiosyncratic personality, or lack of same.

Broadly speaking there are certain distinct types:

a.   The ones who are disinterested, fiddle knowledgeably with switches and dials, pronounce that you need a whole new appliance or system, and leave.

   With him you ask what does he advise, what make, style, price, guarantee, delivery and what will he give for the old appliance, and even more important will he take it away free of charge.

b.   Those who point out it's a poor machine, needs spare parts and was a mistake to buy. "You were sold the wrong one."

   Let him ridicule the appliance, saying it was a disgrace to sell it to you. You can suddenly remember you bought it from his firm, and he fitted it.

c.   The man who stays all day, effectively trapping you in the house. Curiously he needs to go to "the van" frequently to get a tool which you never see him bring back. He also has genito-urinary problems – well

45

definitely urinary problems which may result from the frequent cups of coffee he takes. He has early on stipulated he does not like tea, and it's milk and three sugars. With him you are certainly trapped. Stay in the same room, set up the ironing board and listen to serious radio programmes, preferably about religion, the state of our prisons or even Greek mythology.

d.   The expert who gives you an erudite/ incomprehensible or simplistic lecture/explanation on spin cycles, gravity, messages transmitted by the airwaves, clockwise is the opposite of anti-clockwise and how it is important to switch on "like this" also what happens when hot air meets cold air (the answer LOLA is steam) and above all it is important to switch off "like this". He may read large chunks of the 20-page instruction book to you. Hint – you find reading difficult.

Short of blasphemy he is difficult to deal with. But when he asks you to sign, do so adding B.Sc. Hons Physics/Electronics, Lecture in Computing Science. Litigation lawyer is taking it too far, but Ph.D. in Psychology frightens and does the trick.

e.   The one who doesn't turn up as arranged between 8am and 8pm, but swears later he rang the bell three times. He's not sure when he'll be able to come again – pressure of work.
Open a bottle of wine and go on, call him a liar.

Asking for a new appliance to be installed opens up additional problems. It usually means you need two other machines to make it work. e.g. with a fax it transpires you need an extra phone line; a new phone which cannot be carried away from its place of rest, a new hole in the skirting board for the flex, rewiring, not to mention moving the furniture. Curiously they often ask you LOLA for a screwdriver or torch, or they say a knitting needle will do.

All this is no guarantee it will work. You now have an

unintelligible answering machine and a clock stuck at 1.13am. When you do get it to work, you discover too late that your friends and relatives don't have a fax machine, so you use it only four times year = £52 per fax. Delivery by taxi would have been cheaper, or delivered by courier, but LOLA it's been not just fun but an experience.

WINDOW CLEANERS are less problematical. They always turn up – more often than needed! They tend to "do" the outside before announcing they've arrived, so check on this. Follow them everywhere, room to room and don't be shy. Talk non-stop, and point out smears, any spills from the bucket, and warn about damage from the ladder every time he moves it. LOLA don't forget to make it a prix fixe.

SUMMARISING GENERAL STRATEGIES

1. Don't leave the expert workman alone. Stay in the same room, silent and passive but with arms folded.

2. Alternatively actively ask him at every juncture what he's doing and why.

3. Don't offer tea – but there's nothing to stop you having your lunch.

4. Don't tip. We LOLAs have to learn NOT to tip. Men rarely do. Tipping is a LOLA personality defect.

5. Crucially ask his full name and address; his work telephone number, home telephone number, mobile, and where he's going next. In addition ask who to contact in an emergency – you may have to call him at 2am because the noise of the new machine is keeping you awake. Also get the name/address/ telephone number/email of his immediate boss and the firm's Chief Executive. WRITE IT ALL DOWN. You can then offer him a cup of tea but he'll be in a hurry to leave.

LOLA you might deduce from all this that you need a casual or resident man or husband. You do NOT. It solves nothing, as he will be even less reliable, take longer, flood the kitchen and you will have to buy a whole set of tools, a hose and a longer ladder or even scaffolding.

It is with a certain nostalgia that I remember the days when we had no appliances. We were real domestic goddesses, true slaves with nothing breaking down. That was before science, sophistication and style took over as well as 'the Joneses'.

DIALOGUE. THAT WAS.

Nurse: One last push and you're there.

Mother: I've been doing a last push for the last 2 hours (silly bitch, I bet she's never had kids. I bet no one's ever fancied her).

Nurse: You're not really trying, are you? (I'll be here for ever with this one – and Gerald's got a slap-up meal organised for tonight – with bed to follow, his wife's gone to her mum's.)

Mother: I'm trying. Really trying.

Nurse: (Poor dab! She's toiling, I didn't really mean "one last push" but it helps to say that early on. In fact, I've got time to nip to the canteen for a cuppa and a fag.)

You're not giving up, surely – your husband's mother phoned, wanting to know if she's a granny yet. They are all waiting for you to turn up trumps and produce a beautiful baby.

Mother: It's coming.

Nurse: Just a minute, I'll be back soon.

10 MINUTES LATER

Nurse: Oh, you naughty girl, here's the baby – why didn't you say, you should have told me it was coming.

No need to push – STOP, STOP. Just do what I say. Here we are. I've managed it at last. A girl! Another girl, we've had nothing but girls all this week.

Mother: Is it alright?

Nurse:	Give me time, you took us by surprise. You should have rung the bell, you'll get me into trouble.
Mother:	Is she fine?
Nurse:	Here you are, see for yourself.
Mother:	You are beautiful and mine. I will be a good, good mother. I promise.
Nurse:	Right! Back up to the ward, NO, NO, I'll take your baby.

2 HOURS LATER

| Nurse: | Your husband phoned to say "clever girl". Now, what did he say – oh yes, he said he loves you. He'll be in to see you. |

NEXT MORNING

Nurse:	That was a good sleep. You'll need all the rest you can get.
Mother:	Is my baby alright?
Nurse:	Ward Sister will come and talk to you.
Mother:	Has my husband been in?
Nurse:	Yes, he's with the doctor.
Mother:	Why?
Nurse:	All fathers see the doctor. I'm going off-duty now.

DOCTOR COMES IN

Doctor:	I'm Dr Fisher. I've not met you before, you're looking very well. I've been talking to your husband. I'm afraid he's very upset.
	If I said the words "Down's Syndrome" to you, would you understand?
Mother:	No
Doctor:	Well I want you to understand.

Mother:	Where's my husband?
Doctor:	He'll come in soon …
	Because your baby has Down's Syndrome.
	You didn't have the test?
Mother:	No.
Doctor:	Were you offered the test?
Mother:	Yes.
Doctor:	Ah …
	Do you have any questions?
Mother:	Will she walk?
	Will she talk?
	Will she earn her own living?
	Will she get married?
Doctor:	Hang on, she's a bit young for that. A bit early to be planning a wedding.
Mother:	Will she die?
Doctor:	We've had to take her into intensive care.

(BLEEPER GOES OFF)

Now Mrs McDonald, there are many Organisations to help you. Sister will give you the addresses. Your daughter will be a bit slow but will be a great joy to you and your husband – God's Gift as they say, and who knows, I might see you in the maternity unit again next year.

Ah! Here's your husband.

Interview

TRAGEDY

What a tragedy the fire next door.

> Not really. 'Twas his own bloody fault.
> BOOZING and SMOKING.

Everyone in the street must be SAD.

> Not really.

It'll be an emotional funeral.

> Not really.

Well thank you, Mr Harrow, for talking so movingly about your neighbour.

> He was my uncle.

Back to Huw in the studio.

REUNIONS

An invitation to a Grand Reunion is inevitable now that you are a LOLA. Don't get anxious. Decide immediately whether to go.

<u>DON'T</u> if:-

> You've had a conviction
> You've been detained by Her Majesty
> Are bankrupt
> You have outlived 3 husbands
>
> or   if the plastic surgery was not a success

<u>ACCEPT</u> with alacrity if:-

> You are RICH
> You've got an O.B.E. or similar or better
> You are well-known on The Media
>
> or   Plastic surgery was a success

Having decided to attend, prepare with military precision – fabulous clothes and jewellery indeed ostentatious, having indulged in all the therapies for weeks before.

Remember LOLA you must feel strong and secure enough to cope with:-

1.   Questions about yourself – No need to be truthful
2.   Envy – They are not being truthful
3.   Relief you didn't marry him
4.   Regret you didn't marry him
5.   Resentment that SHE married him
6.   Pride in being superior
7.   Depression and Inadequacy because you are inadequate

Never say   "You look old" or

                "Did you put weight on after having children?"

                "Blonde is better on you than before"

Unless it's deliberate.

Under no circumstances start crying, swear, argue, strip off, make a speech or get drunk. If you get drunk you are likely to do all of the others.

All things considered, glad you went.

Another 10 years before the next.

Not many of you left and you won't recognise them – that is if you remember to go.

MY SHOES AND ME

Today is NAMING DAY.

It is not the naming of PARTS, it is the naming of SHOES –
or rather I am reviewing my shoes and I have chosen you as
my audience.

My shoes are intimately related to me. I am intimately related
to them. What I mean is there is an intimate relationship
between us.

I will introduce you to my SHOES. I need to be stoical
because I will share with you my thoughts and associations,
particularly the emotional associations with my shoes. (Ah
yes. Good. I have the tissues at hand, like in psychotherapy.)

I will compartmentalise my shoes so as not to confuse you.

A   The shoes in my house – on the floor, under the
furniture, in boxes and in the wardrobe – indeed to be
found in every room.

B   The shoes in my car.

And

C   Others – anywhere and everywhere.

D   General observations and advice.

Now the IN HOUSE SHOES

1.   Classic medium heel comfies – 4 pairs, all the same
make and style. Isn't it so sensible when you find perfect
shoes to buy them in every different colour. Five or six
pairs. You can't worry about money when comfort is at
stake.

2. Ultra smart high heels. Crippling, but worth it. For weddings you'll need a 2nd pair of shoes for the reception and a 3rd for the ceilidh.

3. Several pairs of SLIPPERS – all incredibly ugly. Why do they make such awful slippers? I buy pretty pastel slipperettes but be careful slipperettes are vicious. It requires great skill to put them on and indeed to take them off. It is not easy to avoid decapitating your foot or strangling the ankle when the elastic springs back with great speed and force. Yes indeed, you have to be fit with slipperettes – there is a lot of jumping about and falling involved.

4. When you go in to hospital, it is useful to have MULES – to be ill one must shuffle about – mules one size too big are ideal.

5. BOOTS – now well in fashion – essential with a mini. I make sure mine are long and have a zip. It is not remotely sexy for a gentleman to have to struggle and endanger his back attempting to get one's boots off (other items of attire – yes – but not boots). Remember the white plastic boots as in *Heartbeat*?

6. SANDALS are a must for impromptu cruising. Flip-flops are still naff and should be forbidden. Never wear open-toe shoes on snow.

7. This red pair was a mistake – bought after a liquid lunch. I cannot recollect which shop, or indeed which town!

8. Another mistake – this kitten heel, bought in a sale – down from £75 to £25. I felt obliged of course to buy the matching handbag for £175. It doesn't even hold a pair of shoes. No bargain there.

9. But look at these darling Jimmy-Choos. They have everything – sling back, shimmering straps and scattered diamonds – my champagne and caviar shoes – one day I'll need them.

THE CAR

At present there are only 5 pairs in my car, and one odd shoe, the mate having fallen out during a hurried change-over from work to cocktail party (yes it's that lifestyle, hence the shoes).

1. A good all-purpose black – ready for any impromptu posh date or party. It is a great comfort to know they are there. You can arrive at the venue – suss out the degree of elegance and go back to the car to make the suitable change.

2. A flat two-tone brown, already battered but comfortable. Kept for driving but I do venture out in them if I decide I'm unlikely to meet anyone I know. It's strange if I do meet an "acquaintance", the comment is always how radiant I look. Beauty is in the feet of the wearer.

3. There is a pair of red canvas sandals – ready for a charity shop but never given. After all they may come in useful.

4. A new pair, still in the box. I've really been too busy to open them. Very expensive as I recall. I'll be able to wear them soon when my husband is on sabbatical. When he comes home, I can say "these old things".

5. Wellies – prominent in the boot. Old-fashioned but bought in Harrods, strangely enough the same day I bought that Armani Jacket for the Country House weekend. The Wellingtons are of course green and dirty – a dry-muddy. I keep them that way.

There was another pair, but alas! when I changed cars the much loved crepe soles were inadvertently left behind. Sad really, they must feel abandoned, but never mind they wouldn't match my new silver E-type.

Be solicitous in automatic cars. It is tempting to use only one driving shoe. But if flagged down by police, getting out with one black flat and one high red, makes it inevitable you'll be breathalysed.

I fear I am overwhelming you. You may even be wondering whether my expert knowledge of shoes is indeed a FETISH – of Imelda proportions.

Not so. A fetishism is "A cult object. An object irrationally reverenced. A non-sexual part of the body but an object or an action acting as a focus of sexual desire". Clearly shoes are not mine. I have other objects/actions and "focuses" which better qualify.

You may think that I cling on to my friends, my shoes; that I cannot bear to part with them and their poignant associations. Cannot say goodbye. But I do dispose of my shoes in a variety of carefully considered ways – admittedly with deep mourning.

1. Of course, I give to CHARITY. Even this requires judgement. You wouldn't give the same shoes to posh Morningside and run-down Craigmillar shops. It stands to reason.

2. It is never wise to give to FRIENDS. They do not appreciate your style, pretend they bought them in Bond Street and ungratefully complain they damaged their feet, even causing first signs of bunions. You can end up paying for chiropody!

3. Mostly I dispose of my shoes while on holiday. My shoes have been left in hotels in Hong Kong, Minneapolis, Dubai, Sorrento and several pairs in St Petersburg (exchanged for vodka and a furry hat) and of course in railway stations. I regret throwing a pair into the Danube, but I got a wee thrill leaving my blue stilettos on the Orient Express.

Yes, I am what you could describe as a designer traveller. Of course, leaving your shoes behind lightens the suitcase and leaves room for the duty-free.

Returning to the CAR. It has been essential in disposing of shoes. My regular and favourite method is to dispose of all kind of shoes in the hedgerows as I drive nonchalantly along. It can be fun:- Throw them out of the window, one at a time and alternate the colours and style. One needs to concentrate for this manoeuvre. Check:

There are no cars behind
There are no cars in front
And a decent size hedge or failing that a ditch.

It is wise to vary the sides of the road so as not to arouse suspicion. It is particularly challenging to successfully throw the shoe across the front passenger seat; make sure the passenger's window is open and then don't hesitate. This manoeuvre is a bigger thrill than changing your skirt at the traffic lights, but with practice you can become expert at both.

Think of all the scenarios conjured up when a variety of shoes are found on opposite sides of the road. Where is the torso?

You will have by now empathised with my caring and loving attitude towards my shoes. They are not just made for walking. All are remembered and loved with a colourful past history, some are now collectors items.

I know I am being too romantic and sensitive, but I like to think that there are hedgerow corners of foreign fields that forever contain my shoes – a little bit of me.

CONFIDENTIALITY

Multidisciplinary Meetings, especially those concerned with the welfare of actual people i.e. Case Conferences, Assessment Panels, Reviews etc. are all too often fruitless. The demon 'confidentiality' precludes useful discussion and provides an unassailable reason NOT to give information, or a good excuse when details and facts are unclear because research or homework has been neglected. Human Rights, Privacy, Data Protection etc. have to be treasured but one can often take refuge from accepting responsibility by virtue of information being confidential. There seems to be a need to guard one's professional expertise zealously – perhaps to avoid censure, scape-goating or to protect one's job, or fears of litigation.

TEACHERS cannot comment on behaviour at school or college and never pass judgement on the family.

POLICE information is much too sensitive to be made public, even when using jargon.

THE HOUSING MANAGER)	Really should not
BUS ESCORT)	hear anything –
CARER)	they cannot be trusted
NURSE)	
HOME HELP)	
DEPT. SOCIAL SECURITY)	

MEDICAL information is much too specialised and important to divulge.

and the SOCIAL WORKER holds the most precious observations not to be shared. Besides she has to get permission from her seniors and might even have to wait until the Assistant Director of S.W. can attend next Spring.

AND it goes without saying that parents especially must be excluded. It is not good for relatives to hear the views of the Team.

A recent example: School Leavers Panel Discussion achieved little for Carol – suggestions were unrealistic.

Mother attended the next Conference (she was not invited but everyone thought the other had invited her). Mother didn't mind everybody knowing everything about Carol, the teachers and bus lady especially should know about her epilepsy and tablets, and the others should know about Dad's drinking and temper and Carol's brother being unemployed.

Carol laughed and said it was OK. She laughs a lot now and likes her room in the new house the Housing man got them because of the rows and she loves the Day Centre.

Good thing everybody knew about Carol because she had her first seizure in school soon afterwards and the teacher was brilliant. So was the bus lady.

Confidentiality is good for Politicians but with people it is sometimes a mistake.

SLIMMING

LOLA you have decided AGAIN to lose weight. This time you mean it seriously. So that's the 1st hurdle dealt with.

However the initial visit to a Slimming Club is a bigger hurdle and is decisive. It can motivate you, or put you off. All too often it goes like this:-

Client: Am I in the right place?

Leader: Yes. Yes.

Client: I wondered because of the hymns – the singing and all that.

Leader: Well it is a Church Hall.

Client: What do I do?

Leader: You've come because of the cheap introductory offer I suppose. Give me just £4.75 and... WAIT. You'd better buy these 2 books and a Free Fat Bar and the folder and the diet chocolate. Buy it now because I'm going early tonight. That'll be another £8.40.

We're busy tonight, so we need to hurry to weigh you.

No. No. No need to take your shoes off.

12.11. My my. That's a lot for a wee one like you.

TARGET 7.12. Won't be easy-peasy will it, but I'm here to do it for you.

We're late starting, so I won't be able to introduce you, but it's very important that I tell you about myself because I'm Audrey.

I will be your guiding light. Your friend. Your inspiration. Your nutritional brain and I'm sure I'll be the one you thank at the end.

Now look at the photograph.

Who is it? you ask.

It's me. I know you find it hard to believe when you look at me now.

The old me. "She" was fat. Dowdy. Unattractive. Very dull.

Well, in just 15 months "she" became the modern, vibrant, attractive, exciting Dynamo that you see.

BUT you have a Mountain to climb. An Ocean to swim. Depression to endure. Hostility to overcome and Temptation ahead.

Not to mention Money to be spent, and a love-life in difficulties. But when you reach Target Weight you'll find new love. Maybe with a new husband (or lover!)

You may need a new job due to the bitchiness and envy of your colleagues but it will be worth it and there'll be bonus points for ME so I want you to succeed.

Now you've all bought the books etc. Because of the popularity of this group in Mary Magdalene Church Hall and my own reputation, there's been a huge number of you, so because of the later start and so much weighing, there's no time to say anything more.

I'll see you next week and I'll tell you more about myself.

LOLA, you didn't have to speak. It's touch-and-go whether you get there next week. Anyway you're strong enough this time to go-it-alone – and it's cheaper. That makes sense.

Interview

CHILDREN IN NEED

(Celebrity with arm around a LOLA)

I know you care about these children. How much are you giving?

One week's pension £49.

Can't you manage more?

How much are you giving? Cos I know you're a millionaire.

HOROSCOPES FOR A LOLA

It is seductive at any age to predict, guess at, worry about and anticipate or dread the future. Curiosity gets the better of us all and even if not addicted, it is tempting to occasionally check one's horoscope. But how naive to assume one prediction suits all. Interpretation depends on age. For the teenager, Love and Sexuality means first kiss or first something with its attending anxiety and dreams. Later it's ACTION ACTION ACTION, with more danger, more anxiety and more dreaming; followed by less action, varying anxiety and dreamless insomnia in old age.

A LOLA has survived the gamut of experiences in all shapes and sizes in varied settings under varying circumstances and with various others. The future does not alarm. She copes. Similarly where money, travel, mood, ambition are concerned, the horizons have changed with old age. The jargon in horoscopes needs to be understood in a more mature and realistic way.

As always I can help you interpret the jargon and relate it to you LOLA.

- *Will come into money*   -   *Winter fuel sub arrives, or a £10 bingo win.*

- *You will experience a loss*   -   *Any of your friends could "go" or you will lose your purse in the Off Licence.*

- *Be careful in love*   -   *Don't marry him. He's after your money. Get another cat.*

- *Uranus is unpredictable* — *Uranus is always unpredictable. Take an umbrella.*

- *Mercury is retrograde* — *Mercury is always retrograde. Stay in bed. Don't speak to anyone. Don't travel.*

- *A Phoenix will rise from the ashes* — *The odds are stacked against you. Things will get worse. Update your house insurance.*

- *The odds are stacked against you* — *Things will get worse. Horoscopes are always right.*

- *Expect a positive outcome* — *Horoscopes are always wrong – and silly.*

- *There's an alliance between Venus and Neptune* — *Two men will quarrel over you. Stay calm. Accept both.*

- *The new moon visits your sign* — *Keep away from friends and doctors. Do not sell your house.*

- *Adventure ahead* — *Gin and tonic in Gleneagles after T In The Park – a remote possibility.*

- *Cosmic activity makes you vulnerable* — *You are too sensitive. Perhaps you are not liked.*

- *The sun has left your sign. Health worries* — *You need another two tablets to add to your nine. On the other hand are you being poisoned.*

•	*Avoid the wrath of the Gods*	- *Give to charity and pray. Hide on a cruise.*
•	*Saturn is aligning to Mars*	- *You'll make a decision about your daughter-in-law. It's her fault.*
•	*Positive Celestial activity between Neptune and Gemini*	- *You're confused. Avoid alcohol.*
•	*The sun is transiting your solar charge*	- *You're too excited. Give up alcohol.*
•	*Pursue New Outlets, recognise new talents, expand your prospects*	- *Chat him up. Increase alcohol.*
•	*You are at a halfway point*	- *Abandon hope. Give your wardrobe to Oxfam.*
•	*Venus meets the moon. There's a proposal of marriage*	- *It will have to be from you – on both knees. Find a ring.*
•	*Taurus echoes your past*	- *It'll catch up with you.*
•	*Extensive fog masks the planets. Not everything is possible*	- *Give up and spend, spend, spend.*
•	*There's guilt about*	- *Confess or emigrate.*
•	*Fiery Mars departs from Aries (or arrives in Aries)*	- *Both are wrong.*

In fact there is a certain comfort in proving the predictions are wrong. Resort to:

TEA LEAVES. Tea bags are full of meaning. They can lie sideways (cringing or apologetic), half-way in and half-way out (indecisive), or near the handle (cautious).

Be careful before attending a SEANCE. You could make a fool of yourself or be frightened to death.

Don't attempt an OUIJA BOARD if you can't spell. Besides your trusted friend will broadcast the secrets you've divulged.

Why not resort to the ever-faithful CRYSTAL BALL. It is always reliable, if you "help" by indicating your status and circumstances (e.g. wedding ring, tracksuit, laughing or in tears, hearing-aid or zimmer) and speak about your family and your worries.

Think seriously about kicking the Horoscopes habit. If you've given up smoking, gambling, prozac and karaoke, then abstinence should be easy. Failing that, believe only the nice bits. Forget or rearrange the planets – after all the cosmos is changing. Global warming and all that. Rely instead on the weather, your bank balance and gossip.

However, as the sun settles, the moon continues to go round and round, the planets stop rushing about and bumping into each other and hopefully no more planets, meteorites and stars are discovered, you can continue to indulge daily, weekly, monthly and annually in the publications if only to read the negative comments and predictions for your friends.

NO REWARD PLEASE

I was such a good child, so helpful to people, not so much to animals but especially helpful to old people.

Mrs Price was over 80 and had to stay in her house because of a swollen foot. I did the fetching and carrying for her and sometimes made the tea and bread and butter. She told everyone how good I was and "rewarded" me every time with a bowlful of buttermilk. That buttermilk! So COLD, so HOT, so SOUR, so SOUR, so THICK, so YELLOWY and with a smell like SICK, worse than parmesan cheese. I had to drink it with a deep, deep, wooden spoon from a deep, deep huge wooden bowl. It took so long to finish. It wouldn't slip down and there was nowhere to throw it away.

Mrs Price watched me with pride and marvelled at my enjoying it, promising me more tomorrow.

I wanted to stop going there but everyone said how kind I was, and her swollen foot was getting worse.

If I said I had a bad stomach she was certain the buttermilk would cure it so she gave me extra. I tried to think up lies in bed at night.

I'll never forget the taste. I can't use a wooden spoon now nor a wooden bowl, not even for salads! And I never drink buttermilk, not even yoghurt, not even cream.

When I do something kind now, I never wait for a reward in case I get it.

ANGER MANAGEMENT

LOLA why bother?

Why not let rip – it can be cathartic. Besides you've been managing it OK for half a century. You've done Fight or Flight etc. You lost every fight and your flights were limited to the Co-op – never to the Caribbean.

So why not decide to enjoy Anger. At your age strong excitements are few and far between. Besides the adrenaline rush exercises your blood pressure and is good for the complexion and keeping the house clean.

Natural anger is cheaper and more readily available than strong drugs with no tell-tale syringes, and marginally better than alcohol, and unrecognisable in blood samples.

However, enjoying one's anger does produce problems – too many apologies required next day or too many "friends" lost. So it's best to keep it under control, at least with the neighbours.

Deep breathing has been tried and tested but it can take a long time and you may faint. That's why fathers find it helpful in labour.

You are too unsteady, and reflexes are too slow for hitting out.

Verbal attacks such as swearing, gossip and spreading lies are very rewarding, but best of all is an Angry Silence. It wins every time. Tears are counter-productive. Why not try something more fashionable and pseudo-scientific? Why not adapt The Naughty Step? Set up a D.I.Y. Naughty Step programme personalised for you – along these lines.

At the first sign of Anger:

1. Identify the symptoms and the cause.

2. Give yourself a warning.

    Allow yourself only 2 angry thoughts before forcing yourself to go to the N.S.

3. You will have decided on a N.S. suitable for your age and infirmity.

    a) Sitting cross-legged on a cushion on the floor is dangerous – even if possible.

    b) Bed is too comfortable.

    c) The garage is too far for you to drag yourself metaphorically screaming.

    d) Standing outside in the front garden is very effective, especially in full view of the neighbours, but it can damage your health.

        So you decide:- Just stand in front of the vibrating washing machine or the freezer (doors open) or in the wardrobe (doors open) or in the bath (empty).

4. How long?

    1 minute/year of age is ridiculous

    1 hour/year of age means 3 days at a time

    So I suggest 1 minute per decade of age.

5. Saying sorry to yourself is not easy. It's confusing, and it's tempting to cheat and forgive yourself too readily. Try and mean it.

6. The Reward must not be too extravagant or you'll become addicted to Anger.

    Suspect you are at risk of addiction if the N.S. is used more than 4 times/day or twice during the night.

    Deal with it by making the N.S. more frightening or make the Reward less appealing e.g. Pickle instead of chocolate.

A new duster instead of a Lurex "Top"

Sparkling wine instead of Champagne

Sparkling water instead of wine.

7. You must keep a colourful designer CHART in the kitchen. Tell visitors it's a record of your good deeds and charity donations.

LOLA if you don't have an "Anger wall to climb" you can use the N.S. for:

Over-eating
Over-drinking
Over-partying
Over-spending
or Over the other thing

Naughty Step therapy can sometimes take years, but the D.I.Y. variety can be designed with pleasure in mind.

ANNUAL GENERAL MEETINGS

Autumn seems to be the season of fruitful AGMs. Why are they concentrated around November/December? Surely not every organisation/charity/association started in November.

If you choose not to attend, be sure to send apologies or your name won't be in the Minutes. Don't do this for two consecutive years. If you feel the need to give an explanation, make it foolproof. I suggest:- unavoidable absence (unspecified). Family celebrations – not your own birthday obviously. Broken bones – risky – make it a sprain. Date clashes with other Charity, Round Table/ P.T.A/ Weavers group of which you are Honorary President, or opening of a unit of any disadvantaged group. DON'T resort to DEATH of a loved one. You'll get cards of condolence and you might forget next time which one indeed died. Send a Proxy Form. It's less confusing if you give carte blanche to the Chairman, and it indicates you can trust him.

But – if you attend you must READ everything:- last year's Minutes and the dreaded financial report; Profile of Board and Committee Members; Agendas and Items relating to. Read the whole lot 24/36 hours before the meeting. If earlier you'll have forgotten everything. Architect's drawings, Building reports, Health and Safety recommendations, are a mystery to you. I suggest you read the first and last page of Financial Reports and highlight bits you don't understand; or don't read – because you'll get depressed. Never ask a question you know nil about, unless it's a point of grammar. We LOLAs are experts at grammar and punctuation. Be sure to take all documents to the meeting with bits conspicuously highlighted whether you've read it or not.

With your expensive hearing aid you can sit in the back or half-way. Surprise, surprise, 3 out of 4 speakers are inaudible. You hear hardly a word (and neither does anyone else!), but a whizz kid of a technician in front jumps up to rectify/facilitate proceedings with microphones. He's satisfied but after five minutes we hear even less. However, we are polite. Say nothing but like everyone else heartily applaud.

Don't propose or second minutes. Someone might point out you were not present.

Find out beforehand about hospitality. You should attend, to make sure everyone knows you were there – besides you're in your best clothes. Government/Social Work and Education and Financial Agencies put on a spread with wine. Charities cannot put on alcohol – bad for their image – but you can join the Committee at their drinks later.

If *après* AGM is not exciting, rush home – another appointment, and that same evening file all the documents, or preferably shred them. There is another AGM tomorrow night. The organisation is certainly fortunate to have you.

Interview

WINNERS & LOSERS

Well we have to say goodbye to the lovely Lorraine who didn't manage to win any points but you don't go away empty-handed, my darling. You have the Weymouth 'Wish you were here' mug and the sachets of tea and coffee to go with it.

You've been a wonderful smiling contestant. Have you enjoyed yourself?

No. A waste of time. And it's cost me a fortune.

Well that's all we have time for. Let's return after the break.

———

Well Betty, you've won this compact washing machine.

I've got a better one at home. I'd rather have the television.

On my show you get what you win. TOUGH!

HOLIDAYS FOR A LOLA

LOLA you have confessed to yourself but to no one else, the advantages of going it alone. You are no longer in employment and sensible enough to be at no one's beck and call, so you can go, or not go, anywhere and at any time pleasing only yourself. The world's your oyster, but having led an exciting adventurous life you will have travelled widely and been to most places. You can pick and choose, especially where you don't want to revisit.

Perhaps China and the Great Wall no longer beckons, although it was nice to be taller than everyone else, and your white hair admired and photographed so much. Ditto Tokyo, Lapland and Santa is irrelevant, and there are some you never, ever, want to see again.

At your age America is unwise lest you become ill and have to pay thousands for the same op Tony got for free. You could opt to refuse treatment and be buried there. Not a bad idea. Your friends and relatives would conjecture.

Another consideration is the jabs. You're like a pin-cushion and you can't remember what you're protected against.

You've "done" Machu Pichu from your armchair, every Buddha looks the same, and you've seen every animal and life-form close-up on TV.

So you prevaricate UNTIL you hear of the holidays of others. The crunch comes when you phone your friends, relatives, neighbours, colleagues, even enemies and find everyone is away either:- on holiday now, coming back from holiday next week, going away tomorrow, packing or unpacking, jet-lagged and in bed, or dining out on stories of holiday escapades. It seems everyone's whooping it up except you. So

LOLA just get jealous and angry. While you are still in a temper BOOK THREE holidays – say a weekend in Arran, a week in Marrakech, and a ten-day cruise on *QM2* (that'll show 'em). Having booked and paid pronto, you will already feel better and refreshed with no paranoia. In fact you don't even have to go now. Losing your deposit can somehow be therapeutic, and inquisitive friends will be impressed by your cavalier and casual attitude.

A Little Old Lady Alone can choose a variety of travelling opportunities all of which can prove life-enhancing.

COACH TOUR. LOLA you won't get lost, you are counted four times a day. However it can be slow. If you leave Edinburgh at 9am for Iona you've still not reached Glasgow by 2pm, having taken the scenic route via HM Prison Carstairs and East Kilbride. A coach to Achiltibuie or the Eden Project is foolhardy. However a week in a coach is a convenient way to dry out, but Ireland or Germany is not conducive. You do run the risk of being "adopted" by that couple who are on their 20th bus tour but it can be a comfort sometimes to follow the herding instinct. At dinner the first evening bare your soul. Decide beforehand whether you are a spinster (by choice of course), widowed, divorced, have sacrificed your life to care for relatives or you have been abandoned or even battered. You can be sure no more questions will be asked of you. A walking stick or bladder problems means you get special treatment – a case of survival of the un-fittest. Allow a gentleman to help you with your suitcase but stay close to it and to him. He's liable to walk off and you won't see your possessions for three days. However, if you've booked via the travel agent, allow it to get lost. You'll acquire a whole new wardrobe.

TRAINS
Are quicker. But avoid the hotspots. Don't go to Blackpool on a holiday weekend – the bottles of water that those in the hen party take are diluted with vodka. Don't be tempted by a day trip on the Orient Express. It's not worth it. Go the whole hog

and take the train to Venice. By the way there is a very high step to get on. LOLA you will need to be pushed up.

BUS – DAYS OUT
Comfort yourself with a free trip to Inverness or a walk around Grangemouth. If desperate go to Ocean Terminal and watch the tourists spending money on *Britannia*. (Poor old Queen in that bedroom. I'm sure LOLA your own boudoir is luxury in comparison.)

FLYING
Happiness is turning left at the top of the front steps. I find if you hesitate, look vague and hold up the queue there's a strong chance you will get upgraded. Remember a package or charter is not something you can boast about to friends, but you can exaggerate about delays and luggage.

CRUISE SHIPS
Are a natural habitat for any LOLA. It's well known all the widows say "It's what he would have wanted" and of course he's invested well. Go to everything on board: the singles get-together where you meet the hosts who are dapper ex-army clicking-heels types there solely for your benefit, is a must. Visit every restaurant for every meal. Pick and choose. Drink is up to you. There's always an Olde Englishe pub or a Golden Lion. The Casino is also up to you. I find there are too many women there, enjoying inheritance, alimony or divorce settlements.

Be sure to attend every lecture, film, art auction, dance, horse racing (you may well ask) and fashion parade, and don't miss the "specials" for ladies – flower arranging, fondant cookery and "how to fold table napkins". It's surprising you've reached this age without napkin expertise. Excursions to shore are pricey. Think on it. You can get cheap flights for four days from home to Barcelona for less than a few hours tour from the ship. Do get one impressive photograph taken in the dining room, but yet another in a red life-jacket is not necessary. You've already got three.

I feel obliged to advise you with regard to SPECIAL INTEREST HOLIDAYS:

Gardening. Your fellow travellers will be hardy animals, and accommodation will be spartan – empty university halls in summer are popular. Refrain from asking a gentleman the Latin name for a daisy, or you'll be educated in Latin for the duration. Refrain also from buying cacti to bring home.

Flower Arranging and Cookery Weekends. They go together and are gender specific. You won't find a spare male but you will get plenty of showmanship, and histrionics from the "Artistes". Take your smartest evening clothes and jewellery, not be outdone, and don't be afraid to tell them at length about your frangipan dessert or the arrangement you did with one flower and a chestnut. They raffle the flowers afterwards, so you might find yourself bringing home a sculpted four foot pedestal arrangement suitable for an altar but awkward in a car or train.

Wine Tours. It's an advantage travelling alone, no one will be counting, and no apologising or explaining is needed. Don't pretend to be a wine buff so you therefore need to taste them all. Spitting is not essential. Remember wives don't trust their inebriated husbands with inebriated you. It is wise to discontinue your water tablets for the duration, and it's better not to join in any Community Singing as you may find yourself continuing the refrain (with actions) after the others have stopped.

Bridge/Chess etc. Only couples go. If you are trapped into joining a table, remember risk of D.V.T. and do stand up intermittently and stretch – say every 3 hours.

There's little demand for Drystone-Walling, but I'm told Hillwalking brings its own rewards. Excavating is often fruitless. Anything you find goes to Her Majesty.

Camping. A tent for one is definitely out. You may never be able to get up. Don't go.

Whatever you do and wherever you go take extra tea-bags and don't make bosom friends. If that nice family asks for your address, give your previous one and never give your cabin or room number – not everyone thinks you are too old!

Don't ask a foreign waiter or steward about his family in the Philippines because without realizing it you could have invited him and his extended family to successive Hogmanays.

LOLA you may now have decided that staying at home is attractive. Simulate siege conditions. Stock up with gourmet food, a selection of wines, books and chocolates and splash out on ginseng, selenium, face packs and a foot spa. Then DRAW THE CURTAINS. Mon Repos will be more restful than Bon Voyage – with no Single Supplement.

TELEPHONE SELLING

This is not a popular way of doing business – universally criticised and the caller often maligned with strong words involved. The scenario is familiar. You are at home papering the bedroom, trying a new Chinese recipe, renewing your highlights, or just sleeping if off when:

The <u>Telephone Rings</u>. A new voice is keen to sell you something. It's the nuisance call. You explain you've just installed a new freezer; installed central heating; don't want to test-drive a Renault; don't want free telephone calls between 2.00am and 6.00am or weekends, especially not during February; are not interested in a speaking suitcase nor a commemorative plate showing Red Rum, and you already have 3 atlases of the world. You apologise, then explain, make excuses then tell lies and eventually put the phone down.

What a pity! You are missing out by doing so and forfeiting an opportunity for a rewarding discussion. After all he's a polite enough gentleman and only wants to help. Thank him at once for phoning and excitedly ask pertinent questions. He is so surprised that you now have him captive and can set out to have FUN. Confuse him by irrelevancies, repetitions, and non-sequitors, alternating knowledge with eccentric questions, and interrupting, but all along so so delighted to talk. You must sometimes listen and ask him to repeat that interesting bit he said.

It takes practice to develop these skills but persevere and you will have a nervous hesitant stuttering incoherent "wreck" desperate to get off the line but too fascinated to leave.

It's best for me to give you a verbatim example of an encounter.

Telephone rings. *Yes. Hydrangea House. Mrs Cameron speaking.*

Good afternoon, I'm phoning about a special promotion offer from "Windows R Yours" with extra savings for home owners like yourself. We're in your area and you're a priority name.

Yes, lovely. Hullo. I've just come in from shopping. Bought some lovely things, we are lucky to have a Harvey-Nicks. How nice of you to call.

Have you got double glazing Mrs Cameron – it is Mrs Cameron, isn't it?

Yes, I was a Windsor before I got married, and Thomson with my first husband. What's next I wonder? No more changes planned at the moment.

I phoned about your windows.

Oooh, windows did you say? I've got lots. I've got half double glazing but I leave my car in the garage. Sometimes I leave it in the drive – I'm naughty. It's a Datsun – automatic. I know, I know. Don't tell me off – shouldn't buy foreign.

Well, it's lucky I phoned as I could come round now and give you a quote.

Lovely! My feet are killing me after shopping. It's my shoes. I take size 6, but 6½ in slippers and sometimes 7 but that's for wellies. Don't get me wrong, I'm small really, nothing too big except my feet – like my Gran.

I could give you a quote – won't take me long to measure. I'll be there in 10 minutes.

How kind of you to phone and take an interest in me. My hairdresser does that – and sometimes the Vicar but he's getting a bit deaf.

Yes, I see.

Does it matter that I'm left handed?

No, don't worry, "Windows R Yours" can be fitted to open to left or right.

Are you left handed Mr... silly me, I don't even know your name.

Alexander.

Is it Alexander something, or Mr Alexander?

Mr Alexander.

It must be confusing for you, but you can always say that you are the windows man.

I see most of the houses in this Avenue have double glazing. In fact, all except yours.

There's plenty of money, don't know how to spend it. But I love make-up and beauty things, especially pink nail varnish, pink's my favourite colour. What's yours Mr Alexander?

Black – I suppose. Well, for just £3,000 I could complete the whole house.

Could you? And include the garden shed? It doesn't have windows – only in the door – but it's cold in the shed.

You know you really should protect yourself from draughts Mrs Cameron, not to mention burglars.

Oh, you can mention burglars. We've got AC/DC electricity. You can mention anything, you have a special way of mentioning. Have you thought about becoming a Counsellor – not politics I mean, but helping people. Can I have curtains or blinds?

Either Mrs Cameron, no problem. They'd look nice in pink.

*I know! You could belong to those people in Victim Support –
a Counsellor when they've had broken windows, or
passengers on a train when someone's thrown a stone and
broken a window or in a car. You could mend the window at
the same time. Not everybody's got the personality for that.*

**So I take it you'll be ordering new windows then, Mrs
Cameron?**

*We go on holidays a lot – usually foreign but next month it's
Jersey – not really foreign is it? Would we need to take the
glazing bits out? Are the windows foreign? Not made in
Taiwan are they? Mr Alexander, how do you spell Taiwan?*

T A I W A N

*Oh, that's why Marjorie calls it TAYWAN. Not much call for
windows there I don't suppose but I bought a lovely see-
through sarong there.*

As I said, just over £3,000 would probably do it.

*Oh, the new bed cost nearly that, and it's too bouncy. But
what can you expect for only £2,000? And I don't like the
colour.*

**Well, you wouldn't be wasting your time with us. As I
said, £5,000 would cover it – or £6,000 at the most I would
guess.**

*That's a nasty cough you've got. You need a lozenge. I always
carry a lozenge, and I always carry a spoon. You'd never
believe how handy a spoon can be. Would help with your
windows I'm sure, or if you had a ladder stuck.*

I'll give you a quote. I can be with you in 10 minutes.

*You're very decisive. I like a decisive man Mr Andrews, sorry
I mean Mr Alexander. You sound like Mr Andrews. He's from
Newcastle. He's decisive too.*

Yes, it's best if you order windows soon. See you soon.

I'll have a cup of tea ready and a doughnut. Do you mind long-life milk? Pity Mrs Crolla's not here. She might like double glazing. She's got good taste. She'll be back in three weeks from the cruise. She lives here – and no mortgage.

I thought you owned it?

Oh NO. I just come to bring the clean laundry. I'm lucky. If I hadn't come today I wouldn't have had this nice talk with you. It's really made my day. You're a very special man.

Mr Alexander, be careful on the slippery steps.

Mr Alexander, Mr Alexander! Dear me. We're cut off.

LOLA you get the idea. Be friendly. Don't let him go. After all you're not out to seduce him. He phoned you. There won't be heavy breathing. More quick, quick short breaths, with a hint of a stutter, and sometimes long pauses as if he's confused and doubting his sanity. You will be cheering him up.

Other interjections I can suggest to keep the conversation going – half an hour is best:

6. My husband's got eczema. I expect you've got lovely skin, protected by all those windows.
7. That's a nasty cough you've got. Stress I expect. Have you thought of valium. I swear by it. That's a figure of speech. I don't swear.
8. And I'm frightened of bees. Mister A. don't mention bees. Quick, say something soothing to calm me down.
9. You asked something very perceptive. Ask me again.
10. Have you got grandchildren? Silly billy me. You sound much too young and handsome.
11. I've got bifocals. Best to have 2 pairs.
12. My husband is kind but he's got no desire. You need desire don't you Mr A.

13. You don't sound like a mince and tatties man – more tiramisu.
14. You've got a lovely manner. You can't learn that.

A coup-de-grace at the end is so important and very satisfying. Example: If it's a conservatory man, say you're four storeys up; if it's a garage man you've just given your car away; if it's kitchens your caravan is lovely; if it's carpets you're moving house. Any permutation is allowed.

Best wishes LOLA. Cultivate this unique style. It's heady stuff and well worth the telephone rental.

ROUND ROBIN

A garrulous six-page Round Robin is the perfect medium for LOLAs at Christmastime. November is a bit late to start being creative. Ideally you should have started mid-January, and keep dates and details at your fingertips. If not you can just conjure them up with impunity. None of the recipients will have the audacity to correct you. Only the brave would question a LOLA's memory and recall of events – imaginary or otherwise.

So prepare your Round Robin Epistle well. It has to be a masterpiece as it's destined for:- close relatives, less close relatives, faraway relatives, ex-es, in-laws, neighbours of all the houses you've lived in, friends you like and especially friends you don't like, members of every committee you've been on, also charities, the bank, selected people from the Church congregation, the B & B in Kinlochbervie, and that nice lady in Jenners who measured you without touching.

Do NOT send to your children's friends – they'll be embarrassed. Nor the teachers – they'll hold it against you. Nor the Inland Revenue – they'll suspect you. Nor the local constabulary – they'll DNA you. Nor the Social Work Department – they'll file you. So discriminate. Think in terms of concrete and personal/emotional outpourings. Remember the more emotional the better. You need to captivate your readers. Put the following headings to remind you:-

Details about the HOUSE are mandatory. Describe renovations, walls knocked down and say the house next door sold for half a million recently and it didn't have a conservatory and only one en-suite. Describe the garden and the pond plants, and en passant say your gardener comes two days a week and he won 'Best in Show' for his radishes.

CARS, the outward and visible signs of success. Also mention the timeshare, the holiday cottage and the mobile home if appropriate.

HEALTH. You can be expansive. Women's troubles of course, but men's organs and anatomy are becoming more acceptable in conversation. Your operations are riveting. Mention the eminent Professor who performed it, and describe the scar in detail. Admitting to Botox or Plastic is entirely up to you.

BIRTHS are equally interesting especially long labours, and the family feuds about choice of names – who wanted what.

MARRIAGES are out of fashion. It's partners now. (Confusing but sometimes more financially secure.) If you did go to a wedding, describe the dress and the cost and the gift list stressing the kilts were not hired.

You are right about your boss. He's divorced now. You knew it wouldn't last. You said so all along. Gloss over this.

DEATHS AND POLITICS. Don't itemise. Leave them out. It's Christmas after all.

ADULTERY is interesting. You can't believe it of Frank, but what was he doing in a Holiday Inn in Scunthorpe in February? Makes you think, because he lives in Bodmin.

ACHIEVEMENTS. Go to town. Mention everything. New jobs, the perks attached, the car allowance, redundancy lump sums. There must be someone with a Double First and someone's child who's won a Bonnie Baby Competition. Be economical with the truth and especially economical with the untruths.

VISITORS. You've been inundated. You're glad you had the two extra bedrooms and the Aga. That couple you met in Melbourne in '85 came. Never thought you'd see them again. They stayed for three weeks. You had to tell them to go because that widow and her friend you met in Seville was coming. They stayed a month but were no trouble and they brought a bottle of wine every night.

HOLIDAYS. Had two lovely days in Skye. Plenty of rain. The *QM2* was not ideal for LOLAs – too many couples celebrating. A long weekend in York was OK, but aren't the Vikings boring. What did they do anyway?

Up Helly Ha is the best bit about the Vikings. Next year it's Botswana and a weekend with the monks in the Holy Isle. It's good to reinvent yourself annually.

You must mention Christmas. You're not having a Norwegian Spruce in the hall this year. You're going for designer twigs and designer baubles, and giving no presents. You're buying a Goat and a Nurse, for abroad.

Lest your Round Robin sounds too boastful, with a tendency towards gloating, it's best to end on a self-deprecating note e.g. "I'm still a bit of a crock", then you can redeem yourself by saying "but I've lost two stone in weight and look wonderful" with a new wardrobe just in time for Christmas parties.

To send this Epistle you'll have to pay for fifty stamps, but you'll save on the Christmas cards, and everyone will be thrilled to read every page of your news. The Vicar might even thank you in Church. A Round Robin is so worthwhile.

I forgot to say please feel free to enclose photos, perhaps of the conservatory – three-tier wedding cake – bonnie baby, the new bathroom – a distant relative in cap and gown, and the curtains in the back bedroom.

Time to sign off. It's been lovely to chat.

FUNERALS

It is presumptuous and reckless of me to ask a Little Old Lady Alone (LOLA) to please plan your own funeral. After all, this is your final opportunity to be in control and in passing (away so to speak) get your own back. You will have waited a long time, so do not rush the arrangements. As always I have guidelines for you. Tick these guidelines off as you go along.

THE DATE is not negotiable. You cannot commit yourself, but do try and avoid any strike or work-to-rule among the refuse collectors or mortuary staff.

Decide pronto if it's BURIAL or CREMATION. With burial you can be boring or original. Maybe in a woodland with a tree planted on top of you. You can buy the tree now – there's usually a sale at Dobbie's, or at Sea – alone or with a following flotilla. Or in the garden or in your favourite car. It can be anywhere. ASHES however have the advantage of being portable and can be taken by car, train, air or sea – even bicycle. Decide now where you want to be scattered. Better than being kept on the TV or the mantelpiece until the family decides or you're accidentally "LOST" in some unexpected way.

I must update you. There will soon be an import from the U.S. It is the process called RESOMATION (Greek RESOM = rebirth of the human body).

LOOK AWAY NOW IF YOU DON'T FANCY BOILING.

It is eco-friendly – no harmful emissions, uses less energy and there is no wooden coffin to destroy. Your loved ones get the white dust, your bio-ashes, after the silk coffin is boiled with chemicals for 3 hours. I quote "Water Way to go". There are already Resomation Roadshows taking place. Keep a look out.

There are other important decisions to make.

THE COFFIN. Now this is a dilemma common to burial and cremation. There is such a choice these days! Starting with the cheapest there is:- cardboard, but mourners can tell; poor quality wood and plastic handles. Why not? Nobody checks; luxury top quality wood with proper brass handles – shows how much they care; or a Pod shaped to your own body. Very stylish. It's going to rot, so what the hell, or it's going to be burned.

FLOWERS. Either nil (one rose on the coffin looks poignant). Or go the whole hog with flowers everywhere. No in-between. Before adorning the hearse with your name and flowers, consider whether you can reduce the cost by shortening your name. Elizabeth can become Betty, Euphemia can become 'Effie', Marionetta becomes 'Nettie' and Angelina becomes 'Angie'. A nickname such as 'Pip' or 'Star' is OK and a talking point. But not 'Fatty' or "Dotty'.

THE SERVICE. As this may be only the third time you've been religious – Christening and Marriage being one and two – you will not find a member of the Clergy who knows you intimately (unless of course…).

So do without the Minister and be different. There is Humanist/Quaker/ Atheist/Hymns only/even Silent.

The important bit is to make sure all your best qualities are recited in a clear voice. Choose your best friend now to eulogise (don't trust a woman, especially when you're dead) and tell HIM exactly what to say, and much more important what NOT to say. He must avoid phrases such as "Popular with the boss or secretary". "Had to spend a lot of time at conferences away from the family". "Sacrificed achievements for CARING" and please no reference to alcohol or drugs or any convictions. But "Easy with money" and "Generous" is

OK and reference to meeting the Queen or minor royal, Nelson Mandela or the Pope is essential. Failing any of these an Olympic medallist would do – doesn't have to be a gold – or Kirsty Wark or as a last resort a politician. LOLA there is always someone among your friends with an MBE. To be entirely sure, write the eulogy yourself now. You can leave out those episodes in Dublin and Dubai, and no mention of 'Robert', 'Marcus', 'Andrew' etc.

If you've got no one to praise you just get a CD of 'I Have a Dream' or 'And Death Shall Have no Dominion'. No one will understand but the vibes are perfect. Everyone will love it and admire your embracing sensitivity.

MUSIC. Do please keep it semi-religious at least. Amazing Grace, Abide With Me, Bread of Heaven or Bob Dylan is fine but 'Here We Go Here We Go' is just ugly. The Welsh National Anthem is perfect but God Save The Queen is not allowed.

Why not go for a PRE-PAID funeral. It's an investment. Inflation is irrelevant regardless of how long you have to wait before "the end" and it reduces your Inheritance Tax. But be careful. Prices vary. Get at least 3 estimates and 3 references – obviously from satisfied relatives not satisfied customers. Try and decide at least WHERE you plan to die. The office in Scotland charges more to take you dead to Weston-Super-Mare. It's cheaper to go ahead alive. That's where timing is so very important.

Book only ONE limousine. Your children will be on far-flung expeditions unaware that you've gone, and relieved not to have to travel home for such an important, but fleeting, occasion and the neighbours can find their own way. You've done enough for them. So pay for just one. There's nothing worse than an empty limousine.

Let the relatives quarrel about who's entitled to the front pew and who stands where in the 'kissing queue' at the exit. Vociferous quarrelling about arrangements for the tea party/wake/celebrations afterwards (church hall, family home, posh hotel, local pub, or nil) is essential, indeed therapeutic. After all you mustn't make it too easy for your grieving relatives. Don't deny them the bickering.

LOLA, after you've planned all this you will quite suddenly feel remarkably fit and well. Liberated and ready to outlive most of your relatives and friends.

P. S. My sincere apologies if I have been, without of course realising it, insensitive in anyway.

WHEN I WAS RELEASED

It was a Tuesday. I think it was a Tuesday.

It was in September. I think it was in September.

It was in the chemist – the big one.

It was next door to Marks – the big chemist next door to Marks.

It was a hand on my shoulder. It was a big hand.

It was 2 hands – 2 big hands.

The man said I was going with him.

"Fine," I said. *"OK,"* I said. *"I've got a bus pass,"* I said. But we went by car – not far.

A policeman said, "What's your name love?"

"It's Constance."

"Right Connie."

"No it's Constance."

He said something about shops. "You've been shopflitting – shopfishing – shopping – shoplifting."

"Yes I have," I said.
"No I haven't," I said.
"Maybe," I said.

"We're the police, love."

"I've paid my gas bill," I said, *"and my insurance,"* I said. *"And the big one was the poll tax,"* I said.

They were very nice and said, "We'll contact people for you. Your husband?"

"No. He's my brother. Don't, he's got dementia and gets upset."

"Your son?"

"He's taking schoolchildren up that big mountain in Africa."

Your daughter?"

"She's dead."

"A friend?"

"Yes I've got two good friends. Janet – she's lovely but she's in hospital with thrombosis, and my neighbour. He switches his phone off."

"Well we can't go searching all night. We'll keep you in."

"That's fine," I said. *"Company for me."*

It was two nights but I didn't have company. Then they said I was lucky to go home and be forgiven. They said the word pardon and wrote down "released".

I think in the shop they must have chosen me for something in the shop.

I don't go shopping no more.

I don't go out no more.

They say I am released. That must be good.

Interview

OGGI, OGGI, OGGI

Well now our next contestant Roger.

No it's Arthur.

Right it's Arthur – who comes from Southsea I believe.

You believe wrong.
I'm from Swansea and proud of it.
Oggi Oggi Oggi.

*Well done. Maximum points and a cheque for £1,000.
How will you spend it?*

Bingeing and women.

RESOLUTIONS

I have given guidelines and good advice to you LOLA on travel, wills, beauty, finance, funerals etc. You are now in control and ready with your resolutions for the next year. Most important is not to get depressed. Plan your successes and failures to avoid surprises. Then don't waver, be decisive and realistic. You know you. Why not make next year a landmark year – your final shot at perfection.

As a preliminary get into the *Je Regrette* mood. If it's *RIEN*, it means you're lacking insight. Lucky you. More likely to be *Beaucoup* or *le Tout*. So make a list of the less desirable aspects of your past, the longer the list the better, say twenty or thirty regrets and tackle them all. It's multi-tasking. The big ones are obvious like smoking, dieting, etc. It's the smaller irritations that count e.g. forgetting to put the bins out, going to bed still with make-up on and more subtle changes are needed. Alongside is hopefully a longer list of aspects which are admirable, successful, well-adjusted amounting to the real fairly perfect you. This list is kept by your bed.

Look back, around, and forward. LOLA do you not wish you'd done less talking/crying/arguing/phoning/polishing/cooking/housework/apologising and being polite to friends you don't really like.

And more laughing/loving/reading/sleeping etc.

Be realistic. It's too late to get a pilot's licence, climb Everest, become a pop star or win the Nobel, but now is the time to put right the negatives and the gaps. Tailor the list to suit you, to remind you and then tick them off.

Why not:-

Watch more sunsets, spend more, be selfish, deny problems, forget politics, be firm but seductive, agree with everyone or be critical but forgiving, accept invitations to the USA, declutter, eat exotic foods and impose on relatives.

Divide your resolutions into four groups:

1. Those you break during the night between January 2nd and 3rd, saying you resolve to wait until Lent to give up smoking/drinking/gambling/eating. Etc.

2. Those you'll keep until January 12th's party. Well done.

3. Those you decide it was a mistake and silly to consider. How right you are, and

4. The one or one-and-a-half you succeed in keeping. What strong will you have.

Include only one difficult habit but five or six from your easy list. They'll make you feel good and motivated when you succeed, and you can tell family and friends that you made twenty-two resolutions and kept sixteen.

As well as the big decisions, have the courage to change in other ways. Throw caution and servility to the wind.

Give opera a miss. Forget culture. Go to the pantomime instead.

Have that extra glass of champagne.

Refuse to go to Part 1 and Part 11 of *Ivan the Terrible* on the same day.

Accept all invitations and stay overnight.

Say 'No' to guests especially the non-paying kind. You are full over the next Edinburgh Festival.

Answer back or more aggressively stay silent.

Never make another *'gateau le progrès'*.

Those are the real fulfilling resolutions, so it's worth failing one or two of the others. You will lower your blood pressure, and make different friends. You will stride the world like a Mrs or Ms Colossus. If you fail the others, care not. You will have learned from the attempt and will get back to square two.

We are at the third traffic lights on our journey towards anecdotage. Let's keep driving, purposefully and with some speed, but carefully. Bon Voyage. See you en route.

GIVING AT CHRISTMAS

Christmas giving should start with the Advent Calendar. Play it safe. Avoid scenes which are too religious; exclude those with chocolates in the little doorways/windows, so you're left with pictures of birds and animals or a suitable quote. You will be remembered daily by the regular breakfast argument about whose turn to open.

You should have already sent Calendars to anyone overseas who expects a present, or from whom you expect a present. Make sure there's an envelope with any huge calendar. Avoid censorship by restricting yourself to scenes of Scotland.

Well before Christmas decide on subscriptions to magazines. Never send specialist magazines to specialists in that field e.g. Butterfly World/Car Maintenance/Ornithology/Angling/Films etc. BUT *The Lady* is a nice thought for an elderly spinster who must not get excited. *Baby* issues for new parents, but Dr Spock and appropriate Margaret Mead shows class, and anxiety. Why not have fun and send:- *Playboy* to the Vicar in a rural practice; *Hello* or *OK* to your university professor; *Horse and Hound* to your local MP and "Recent Animal Research" to vegetarian friends. All to be sent in see-through wrapping (not brown paper), and to the family home. They will be reminded of you every month and delighted. Explain it's "just a bit of fun".

The rest can be Tokens/Tokens/Tokens/Money/Money/ Money. (It's fashionable to say the topics three times these days. Like Education…)

The above entails no packing, no parcels, no expensive postage, and the amount you send is a good indication of the relationship (duty/habit/guilt, or might even be affection, even love). The advantage of money is: no prevaricating, and no struggling around the shops. That can be dangerous for a LOLA.

So you've finished your Xmas shopping. Apart from the CARDS. Why not decide to send NONE. You will be surprised how many of your friends thank you effusively for the card you didn't send. Be mischievous and ask was it the Robin or the Breugel skating scene you sent. Almost all will say the Robin – it's better known and easier to pronounce. After this positive experience you'll never bother with cards again.

To receive gifts requires more subtlety. LOLA you too would like but won't get tokens or money – they don't want to insult you. So it's bedsocks, bedjackets and hot water bottles again. You've now got 22 bedsocks but still only two feet. Be magnanimous and tell the giver you can't have too many and the bedjacket and hot water bottle cover is a new kind of pink to you. It's as if they expect you to spend all your time in bed or in hospital.

Perfume is marginally better. All your children, grandchildren and neighbours have given you perfume, bought on the flight home from package holidays. A rough estimate would be 9 x 3 = 27 holidays = 27 perfumes, so it's difficult to look pleased about another L'Air du Temps. You long for "Evening In Paris" in that little blue bottle you were given when you were young and in love. And you have enough SOAP to eradicate all government SLEAZE – metaphorically speaking.

LOLA because you nave been so kind and generous over so many years everyone asks you what you want because "You have everything". How stupid can you get, but you have the dilemma of how to respond.

- Don't say "Please don't bother, anything." You'll get rubbish like last year.
- Ask for something specific e.g. a garlic press – you've never had one; a Victoria Wine selection; the

Complete Works of Jane Austen – shows refinement; a cruise, or failing that a week in Tomintoul – it's a nice name and you'll be the first to get snowed in every winter.

- Fountain Pen, and ink. Virtually unobtainable these days.
- Best of all say you know how much they care for you, and would want to give, so because they are so busy you've bought their present to you already, to save them the bother. LOLA thereby the world's your oyster. Keep the receipt.
- Never be tempted to specify a brand of chocolate/chutney or marmalade you like. It's salutary to remind you of an elderly friend (male) who fifteen years ago inadvertently said he enjoyed Stilton. He's now surrounded by blue jars and hates the stuff. No one thought to send him the port to accompany it. A glass or three would have given him the courage to throw the cheese away, untouched, in the porcelain.
- But the very best of all, say you'd like the services of a personal Tutor to explain:- your digital radio, washing machine, mobile phone, video, the radiators, the fax, the sorbetière, text messages, e-mail and all the extras you've been told to buy. Tell relatives to club together and pay for a young man, or even old man to fulfil these requirements. He can come between Christmas and New Year when it's quiet and he'll have more time. Make him your best friend.

LOLA follow all this advice. Don't be swayed. Tot up the money saved. Thank everyone in advance. Make it socialising not shopping. It's a good Yule Tide. WORRY YE NOT…

RETURNING PRESENTS

This should be hassle-free. It's a considerable art. Master it as you may want to exchange or take all your presents back. GO EARLY – if possible Xmas Eve. They are too busy with queues of harassed foolhardy men to ask questions.

Explain as little as possible. Just saying "It's no good" often does the trick, but you might need to have a selection of "reasons for returning" ready.

Examples:

Mobile phone	Can't understand how it works.
	I'm allergic to the colour.
	It doesn't fit in my evening handbag.
Food	It looks/smells OFF.
	I can't see the sell-by date.
	I'm going away and not back until after the sell-by date.
Radio	I can't get Radio Forth or SAGA.
	The manual is too complicated – take it and ask them to read it.
Underwear	Wrong size/colour/shape.
	Boyfriend doesn't like it now.
	Brandish it to the man behind – ask his opinion.

Try not to say:

> I've only worn it once.
> Boyfriend gave it to me and I finished with him at the office party.
> I'd rather have the money.
> Look at it. It's really ugly.

I've got another one just like it.
Tangerine is not my colour.

Before giving up, sign a complaints form and put "Lawyer"
brackets.

Keep trying until Easter and you're sure to succeed.

LAST WILL AND TESTAMENT

LOLA you are a responsible person and will have made a Will, even if it's a panic-quickie at an airport witnessed perhaps by a Jamaican and an Irishman. There is no longer a £2 Post Office 'quickie' – it's now £9.99 at booksellers. But beware - if you anticipate post-death difficulties from an 'in-law' or your ex's family, do something more substantial. There are often special offers – free Wills from solicitors with charities benefiting. A shrewd move on their part because you are then captive so to speak regarding codicils, changes, power of this that and the other, and have to pay the full price.

I must at the outset tell you that there is something new and exciting to 'enjoy' now before you die and is becoming more and more popular. It's the "LIVING WILL". It gives you control, inasmuch as you can decide now who will have the authority when you're "nearly there" to:- switch you off, starve you to death or deny you treatment. You can see why this person is crucial. I advise against choosing just one individual. Appoint a syndicate – say five people. They'll never reach consensus, so you will just go on and on. Do not under any circumstances appoint a beneficiary of your Will. Why not choose your florist or your favourite TV personality, but it's polite to ask them beforehand. You can ask to be "despatched" A.S.A.P. This is no problem. Alternatively you can ask to live A.L.A.P. (as long as possible). Stipulate what you want: tubes everywhere; someone to talk to you non-stop say in relays (draw up a rota of relatives and neighbours); and which loud music you prefer. It could go on for one year, two years... ... ... BLEED THE NHS. You've contributed your bit. After all brain-dead is a relative condition. You've probably been nearly there at that party in Ibiza, and that reception with free drinks in Dublin. It's not unpleasant, and there might be a miracle – whereby you sit up and ask for smoked salmon.

You have surely LOLA already appointed a POWER OF ATTORNEY or Continuing Power or Registration Of, for your financial affairs, bills etc when you "lose the capacity to decide yourself". There's a Self Help Kit available. It's easy and a responsible thing to do, but don't tell the lucky person whom you appoint, as it's tempting for him/her to expedite or exaggerate your "incapacity". Trust no one.

Composing the WILL PROPER can be thrilling. You now realise your considerable assets, and how many friends you have and the few you wish to remember. Relatives and acquaintances are viewed in a different light. So don't rush it. There are endless permutations. Enjoy the possible fall-out effect, and you can keep changing your mind.

The house, cash, investments, towels and saucepans are the easy bits. The headache comes with:

Jewellery. Have all items valued. This is your opportunity to show favouritism. No need to be subtle in settling old scores.

Edinburgh Crystal. Is loved by foreigners. Give to anyone living in Russia and donate your Thistle Liqueurs to the Japanese Embassy.

Family Heirlooms – nobody wants, so bequeath them to your daughter-in-law. Similarly photographs clearly labelled "not to be thrown away".

Love Letters. Choose to make them public, or destroy them, along with the Ann Summers products. You can be subtle, whimsical and mischievous. There is no redress.

At "The Reading of …" picture the sombre gathering respectfully riveted on every word. So make it complicated with as much hidden meaning as possible. Conjecture, arguments and idiosyncrasies are worthwhile legacies.

You may not be aware that you can make a VIDEO WILL. Isn't that exciting? Dressed in your best, relaxing with champagne, you make direct eye contact and give pithy below-the-belt summaries of their selfish/arrogant/disinterested/ungrateful personalities; at the same time naming those who are kind, caring and sensitive. Avoid rudeness, but little "digs" add interest. Drag up the past. You can add a theme tune, and alter the background shots, even alter your clothes to suit every recipient. You can alternate smiling with tearful, and of course you can update the video at every whim. A whole new hobby has emerged for you, but try and be kind and explain why there's 'nil' for X and Y and a fortune for Z. If you're giving most to an animal charity, illustrate the work e.g. showing Lemurs, Dover sole or a donkey sanctuary.

To conclude! I urge you to start planning now. It can be fun and is therapeutic, especially the chopping and changing depending on your paranoia, degree of inebriation or just on a whim – rational or otherwise.

It is important to review and modernise the document frequently. Read it every three months (every six weeks for the over 70s). Alter when necessary, especially if you inherit further money yourself, and especially if you marry/remarry/divorce/separate or acquire a new co-habitee. Major adjustments are then essential. You will know instinctively what they are.

After what has been a full life, have a full death. You will RIP – your relatives may not.

FIT FOR FESTIVITIES

LOLA there's a hectic time ahead. You need to concentrate on being fit for the shopping and especially the partying. Your Family History regarding your health is vital but beyond your control. You should have chosen your parents and grandparents with more care. You now have their genes. Blame them. Don't suggest it's your glands – they'll have you on thyroid tablets or HRT (again) as well as a full body MRI and copious collecting of blood and waste products.

Then it's diets, exercising and reducing stress. Abstinence is soul-destroying. Weight Watchers has worked for you three times, but look at you now. Besides you've heard just about everything about the leader and her family – her shopping basket, store-cupboard, relationships and photographs illustrating how fat she was and now so slim. Besides Weight Watchers is not a place to meet men.

Strangely when you were runner-up slimmer of the year you were considered an expert in diverse areas, and constantly asked for your opinion on lipstick, the music awards, Big Brother, Tracy Emin, the soaps, vivisection, the Scottish Parliament Building and the fate of seals. As if being an expert at losing weight makes you an expert on everything, just as footballers and their WAGS are popular on things like *Question Time* and quiz shows. Maybe husbands and Girlfriends (HAGS) will in future suffer similar indignities.

Do your own research on vitamins. Take ten a day of A, all the Bs, C, D and E and selenium for three months. Spend a fortune then take nil for three months. Curiously you felt better on nil.

LOLA you can only stay slim if you exercise. Nothing

strenuous. Jogging, diving and marathons are out. TV cameramen love to show LOLAs looking silly in baggy shorts and semi-conscious. And it's a pity to waste your bus pass by walking. Join a Gentle Exercise class for Seniors. Claim a place at the back of the hall and guard your territory. Have a chair handy. After two years you will feel confident enough to lie on a mat, but stay near the wall so that you can get back up. If you sprain or break anything you'll be given drawings of exercises to do, Lowry-like illustrations of standing on one leg with a knee bent and arms in the air. It makes for disharmony at home. Invite the physio to tea and cry. Let her show you what to do. Much simpler is to walk on tippy toes in a straight line – practising this becomes useful when asked to do so by an Officer of the Law.

A word of warning about sun beds. LOLAs tend to get blotchy. Besides some bits will never be seen at your age.

Similarly give health farms a miss. It's too intense for a LOLA. One item of physical improvement per day is enough or preferably two per week. If you do feel compelled to go to a health farm choose one as far away from home ground as possible. You don't want to meet your lawyer when you're waddling about in a dressing gown. Why not go to Budapest or the Black Sea – mud is soothing.

Avoiding stress is more difficult. You will have stacked away money to be comfortable; have a nice house (but only one bedroom so you can't have friends/relatives to stay). Restrict your entertaining. You're allowed to forget you invited guests then ask them to go for an exciting carry-out and be the life and soul of the party at little cost.

The observation that you live longer and are happier if you are married is debatable. LOLA do not remarry. That myth applies only to men who stand to gain in every way.

The perks of being fit are many. You can keep up with other LOLAs, and be more nimble – an advantage when men are involved.

PAMPERING

Yuletide is the season of fruitful parties for LOLAs so we must be ready and prepared. Invitations come in thick and fast. We become visible to others every November/December/January – believing perhaps that we come out of a summer hibernation. In addition to (sometimes) guilty relatives, invitations come from:-

A variety of organisations: Age Concern, The Church, Round Table, Woman's Institute, Rotary Club. All arrange a variety of exciting events.

One can be sure of at least 4 Christmas lunches, 2 pantos, 2 ceilidhs, several outings: to *Britannia*, crystal factories, city tours and the outside of the Scottish Parliament as well as repeated community singing and film repeats of Bing Crosby, *Bambi* and *The Sound of Music*. The school Nativity play is a must, to see your granddaughter as 'Mary' and your grandson – besides you supplied the shepherd's tea towel and the shawl for baby Jesus.

Please go to them all. It's exciting to see LOLAs behaving badly, and don't forget there's an opportunity to meet a variety of men at all of the above.

So be prepared. Have a strategy and concentrate on the main area keeping up stamina, avoiding undue stress and pampering yourself.

Pampering is no longer an indulgence. As a LOL Alone you can make pampering a lifestyle. To be indulged daily, requiring nobody's permission and devoid of guilt. Make a list and start asap. Indulge, give yourself s beauty MOT. This time I do not recommend that you work from top to bottom, but from bottom up.

FEET – fix chiropody and a pedicure. You don't need nail varnish as you should not be wearing open sandals LOLA, but it's lovely to contemplate red toe-nails in bed. A chiropody hazard is slipping with your moistured heavenly feet and it's too difficult to put your tights back on – so take socks.

MASSAGE – take control. YOU choose the body parts you want "done" – aromatherapy, reflexology, hot stones or straight hammering. Allow acupuncture only if you've had it before. Deny all illnesses, otherwise she'll do nothing without a letter from the GP.

Full body – is best value, but you need to direct her (or preferably him) to the bits you like. Neck and shoulders – lovely. Strangely they're not told as students that you've got arms coming from the shoulders. Do not allow your neck to be "pulled". Say you don't like the noise. Also the couch is a hazard: it's a mountain to climb, a balancing act when you're on it, and even more treacherous, getting off. They insist you drink water bless them. The price charged could surely rise to an alcoholic pick-me-up.

FACIAL – yes get the lot done; eyes, lips, cheeks and all the creams – cleansing, toning, scrubbing, exfoliating, anti-ageing (too late), vitamins, luminescing, concealing and hormone. It's not the best time to experiment with Botox, and don't have anything lifted. Respect gravity. Eyebrow reconstruction is risky enough, but if you go before the end of November, your eyebrows will have returned by Christmas Eve! It's a good idea to visit your friends casually or en passant after your facial.

MANICURE – of course. Little diamonds in the nail varnish look silly but a talking point.

HAIR – LOLA play safe. Don't risk anything and don't be tempted by the cheapies on Tuesdays to be a model for students.

CLOTHES – Everything in your wardrobe is back in fashion including the Winkle Pickers, and especially the accessories. Retrieve the items you put in the grandchildren's dressing-up box, and why not get out your wedding dress LOLA – used only once by careful lady owner, back in fashion.

Now all you have to do is get psyched up.

HEALTH ISSUES

Avoid stress by the following:

1. Minimise Christmas shopping. Send no cards – no one will remember.

2. Simplify gifts. Make it tokens, tokens, tokens or subscriptions. No worries. No parcels.

3. No entertaining. You'll be out all the time, so you won't need a tree or decorations. Perhaps something on the front door just to reassure.

Avoid financial stress. Count up your money, spend it and then indicate to the family how you're just managing with food and heating etc.

Research shows there's less stress and more happiness if you're married. LOLA don't be fooled into rash decisions – men benefit mostly from being married. Casual and varied relationships are much better for you.

Stock up with your regular medication with extra painkillers and something for nausea and bloating.

Go shopping without friends. It's less stressful. The benefits of the ALONE bit of LOLA.

There are perks. You can live gratis on turkey and the trimmings from mid-November to mid-January. Besides, no two Christmas dinners are the same but after a dozen or so. LOLA, there is risk of addiction. Take doggie bags for the mince pies and Christmas pudding you can't eat. Choose someone exciting ($\male$) to pull your cracker. Refuse to wear an orange paper hat. Exchange or steal one to match your dress. Don't forget there'll be photographs.

So LOLA party with gusto, aware there may not be many more. Enjoy!

Interview

HOLIDAY

<u>James won last month's prize</u> – 10 days holiday in The Virgin Islands.

What a wonderful prize. You must have had a wonderful time – all that sun and scenery and 5 star treatment. Tell me about it.

It was rubbish.

I know you're just joking. You had your best mate Anthony with you.

We were both gutted.
He thought it was rubbish too.
They should be reported for saying lies.

What do you mean?

Calling it the Virgin Islands – not true.
Rubbish again.

Well thank you both for coming back to tell us about your exciting holiday and show us your lovely tan.

SURVIVING INVITATIONS

For a LOLA the dreaded phrase at this time of year is "What are you doing for Christmas?" Followed by a more alarming and devastating "What are you doing for New Year?"

The truth is you're looking forward to:-

A Sitting with feet up in your new slippers with matching bedsocks. The only taxing decision is which colour to choose out of the three pairs you've been given.

B Sipping a Chardonnay, followed by a Sauterne with the chocolates. You had to buy both bottles and the chocolates yourself – don't dwell on this.

C Snoozing through Her Majesty, but there was nothing new – same hairstyle, same pearls, same brooch, same accent since 1966, same speech but new additions to the family.

D Selecting next year's holiday.

E Soaps etc on TV interrupted by the occasional siesta.

What better way to spend Yule-Tide.

"Tis a consummation devoutly to be wished." But it is not allowed for you LOLA. Too many people love you over the Festive Season – Goodwill and Guilt and all that.

Decide on your excuses in advance.

A You've been invited to relatives – fat chance! Give details of trains say to Bury St. Edmunds including where you have to change, it gives authenticity to the economy with the truth.

B   Relatives are coming to you. Better still say all seventeen are coming to you, so you'll be rather busy.

C   You are manning a soup kitchen. You've always wanted to do it for poor, lonely unfortunates.

D   Go to the Isle of Man or Belfast. Not too far away and they're cheap. Hopefully there will be a strike at the airport or railway. Christmas is a good bet for a strike.

E   A murder mystery weekend in a hotel is tremendously emotional. You won't need to talk to anyone, as you will suspect all fellow guests. Make a request beforehand not to be murdered. It ups the blood pressure.

F   Spend all day on a train to the Eden project, but be sure to check if it's open.

G   Go to a retreat, preferably run by silent order of monks.

Similar plans should be ready for Hogmanay. What is worse than a knock on the door or a kind phone call at 11.30pm to invite you to a party. You grab something casual only to find it's little black dress time with sequins.

You wouldn't dare leave Scotland on New Year's Eve so the only option is to draw the curtains, put the lights out, have TV on very low (wearing your hearing aid) and oblivion, or go to bed early with Bolly and write your own horoscope.

I've never appreciated the need to take a bottle to friends and then ask for it back to take to the next house and where do you find the coal these days? However you can recruit the tall dark man in advance and decide to stay at home.

After the festive events, you can say all your plans fell through but luckily you had vegetarian sausages and mini-chips in the freezer. Also some ice-cream; and you cheered yourself up by phoning your son in Tokyo. They were enjoying themselves with HER parents. All your other relatives were inebriated and happy.

Try not to resent them LOLA. Be snug indoors safe and sound, solitary and secure and secretly satisfied.

MARIAN – 30 next birthday

Address: Silver Lodge Care Home – Youngest Resident

Staff keep asking me if I'm OK

I always say 'yes'

They ask if I've got everything

I always say 'yes'

They ask me to help in the kitchen

I always say 'yes'

Ask if I like my room and the curtains

Yes

They ask if I want to go on holiday

Yes

With Helen

Yes

They ask me if I like hamburgers

I say 'yes'

They ask me if I'm happy

I say 'yes'

Best to say 'Yes'. They like it. They love me when I say "Yes".

———

In bed last night I said, "Tomorrow I'll say 'No' "

No about the jumper. I don't like green.

No about Hamburgers. Fish is nicer.

No to Holidays – the minibus is noisy.

Helen asks me for money and NO I am not so happy.

I'll say it after breakfast. 'No' I'll say.

———

I DID IT. I said "NO" to my key worker. Not after breakfast – I waited till after tea. She was very surprised and said she was trying to help and do nice things for me because I like it and am so nice and grateful. She asked if I meant the "No" and I said, "No I was only joking and I meant "Yes". I always mean "Yes".

She smiled and gave me a hug.

She said, "Silly you. I knew you were joking."

"I know you mean 'Yes'
I know you are Happy."

She was so pleased.
She likes me.

PREPARING FOR EMERGENCIES

It is wise to peruse all mail carefully before discarding. The most unlikely envelope can prove exciting, even life-saving. Such a document, illuminating and serious, was delivered to me recently.

At first I thought it was junk mail, perhaps to tell me I'd won again! Even the envelope was meant to be artistic – coloured circles with strange hieroglyphics, and with arrows. But no. It was from the Scottish Executive. I took note as their leaflets are always so amusing, especially the one about "Eating Well", although I thought the corn on the cob was a banana. Besides HM Government was printed on the left-hand corner, and one knows this guarantees value for money and is always of vital importance.

"Preparing for Emergencies" tells us all we need to know. Nothing to do with divorce, mumps, stolen cards, midges or thunder, but terrorist attacks were highlighted. However, it can be "adapted for use in many domestic situations". (Alcohol comes to mind.) To summarise the actions required are:

- Find a telephone and dial 999.
- Check to see if you are conscious or if your bones are twisted or sticking out. If your legs don't work don't walk; if your arms don't work don't gesticulate. Common sense really. Wrap yourself in cling film if you're burnt.
- Go inside a safe building. Presumably that means go out of your own house, then cross the road, and walk half a mile to a large building like a cathedral,

dragging everyone with you. But! Do not go into the cathedral if it's on fire.

- Then LOLA you must turn on the radio. I'd go for Radio Scotland, but if Fred McAulay is too frivolous for you, go to SAGA for nostalgia. You may find Radio 4, and can choose between "Poetry Now" or "Life in The Trenches". Wagner's "Ring" on Radio 3 would certainly keep you calm for eight hours or even asleep.

- If you are in your home, don't sleep, it's dangerous it seems. I suppose that's where most people die, and don't go back to bed if it's on fire. Don't use matches or lighter. If a door feels hot, don't open it.

The most difficult bit is the advice to "Stay close to the floor". This requires practice, but you will soon get the hang. After all we LOLAs have spent our lives close to the floor.

The bit about BOMBS is scary but someone will shout "I'm in charge". Follow him. It won't be a woman. They cannot be trusted to take you in the right direction, or park you when you get there. With bomb debris, this time you must "stay close to the wall" and tap on pipes.

Then if you've actually seen the bomb (they should have given a diagram here) tell the police. However, you can be more poignant and it is more lucrative to tell the TV cameras.

The booklet then seems to give conflicting advice.

(a) Look for the safest way out
(b) Stay inside in case there's a second bomb.

What about a third or fourth bomb I ask? Decisions. Decisions.

It also tells you what to do if you're nowhere near your home. They don't mean in L.A. or Australia but out shopping somewhere. Remember, listen to the radio. They are being thorough.

DECONTAMINATION is done by the Fire and Rescue Service. They have been trained. It sounds very personal. A LOLA would not relish the thought of a young fireman "soaping and dressing" her (presumably after undressing). Try to co-operate. After all with all that soap your eyes will be closed.

The Pamphlet refers on almost every page to WWW. LOLAs tend not to use WWW, and have little expertise in controlling bleeding. LOLAs are certainly very suspicious of mouth-to-mouth in emergencies, although experienced in other contexts.

Thank God you've mastered the wireless!

Oh my God! You've realised you don't know how to turn off the water, gas and electricity. Shame on you! Why not turn everything anti-clockwise. They don't mention the lights so you won't be in the dark.

They tell you to help elderly vulnerable neighbours. LOLA don't. You are one of them.

You should gather together "useful things". No! the suitcase you've kept for holidays or emergencies is not reality-equipped. You need useful things.

Start collecting tins of food now – salmon, soup and stews for example. Peanut butter and Marmite will sustain you, and couscous takes up less room than long spaghetti.

They advise taking a bottle opener. You'll be glad to get rid of the six you've acquired. That must mean bottles will be provided, probably spirits of some sort. Water does not cheer.

You'll have a heavy load to carry if you include torch, spare batteries and a phone, not forgetting the all important radio. Also blankets can be awkward. Persevere.

Crucially you must – we all must – "help to catch terrorists", so dear LOLA don't invite them to live with you, and report anything suspicious in your cupboards or dustbin. Now is the opportunity to report any concerns you have about your neighbours – their idiosyncrasies, odd habits and all the comings and goings – giving graphic examples. Perhaps you should now stay close to the window, and watch. With the radio. Curiously there's no instruction to watch the TV.

Study the booklet every day to keep up your blood pressure and anxiety levels – so it's a good idea to keep one bottle opener handy.

Don't have nightmares because you are safe in the knowledge that firemen, policemen and if necessary the Armed Forces are looking after you, not to mention the staff at the Cathedral. Come to think of it the Cathedral is not heavily staffed, and I am not aware of telephone booths in the Vestry, and have never seen or heard a radio not even at Christmas. Perhaps it's hidden in the pulpit along with a cache of batteries. It might be safer to go to a Bank.

On the other hand all entry points into the UK have "excellent state-of-the-art surveillance systems". So why not go to the airport or the docks. Decisions again.

You can get the excellent and very pretty Pamphlet in Audio tape, large print or Braille and in a dozen different languages. Welsh is there of course, along with Urdu, Somali and Gujarati. But what, no GAELIC? Alex Salmond, where are you?

You WILL have nightmares, but don't worry you'll be alright on the night.

We really should say a big "THANK YOU" to the Scottish Executive.

Interview

CABINET MINISTER

Why did you resign from the Cabinet: a year ago?

I wanted to spend more time with my family.

Why are you coming back to Cabinet?

I've had enough of my family.

WE ARE A GRANDMOTHER

Most older LOLAs have considerable experience in the role of grandmother – getting it right and more often getting it exactly wrong. However, many of you will benefit from the following guidelines.

BEFORE THE BIRTH, you will have already behaved impeccably. i.e. no coercion "to produce"; no subtle hints, no advice (equals interference) and no phoning to ask "Has it arrived yet?"

Be absolutely delighted then shut up.

WHEN "IT" ARRIVES either be out of the country, or close at hand round the clock – especially the midnight to 6am part of the clock. Learn how to make tea properly and wear an overall. It indicates your position. Preferably, don't touch the baby.

Carefully consider the following:

GEOGRAPHY – Where to live. I'm in favour of a move, say to New Zealand – just like Scotland, or Helsinki – just like Scotland but less windy.

Don't worry about the cost of visiting. It's probably cheaper (my estimate £2,100) to visit, no frills, from New Zealand three times a year (quite enough) than weekly outings to the zoo, cinema, Sea World etc, along with crisps, drinks, pizzas, chips and the obligatory McDonald's (my estimate £2,575) all-in. Besides they won't be able to visit you often.

If however you stay in the same town, 5 miles out is the worst scenario entailing late transport home, or staying overnight and getting the breakfast and cleaning the house before leaving.

A word of warning. Don't ever sleep on a settee or a futon. It has to be a bed – even if it's theirs – or nothing. Start as you mean to go on, and it will go on. It's a charming idea to occasionally bring a strange elderly man to keep you company.

Why not consider a 'granny flat' and they'll have you around constantly. BUILD ONE – after all you've probably already paid for most of the house. Fit a loud baby alarm and you can have a nice meal, a couple of glasses, in nightie and slippers or whatever! And be bright and cheerful when the parents come home. You must wake up if you're asleep.

MONEY. Give freely even if you have to conspicuously do without. Tell everyone you do not begrudge it. Start with the obligatory Premium Bond. It will never win because it's cashed within six months. Consider Children's Bonds. The parents can't get at it so easily.

A Trust puts you in control, and you can change your mind depending on their behaviour. Do not give the grandchild a cheque at Christmas or birthdays. It's put in the bank, and he'll not see the money until he's in university, and LOLA you might not be around to be thanked. Give a present instead to any child over two. It avoids the other 'granny' winning. Treat all grandchildren equally. The 13-year-old gets much the same as the 3-year-old, but tell every grandchild (secretly) that you like him or her the best.

THE OTHER GRANDMA, is of course your good friend, but outwit her. Constant probing research will reveal what she does for the family, what she criticises or praises, and what presents she gives. Then give the same but a more expensive model, or give the artistic opposite, and it must always be 'educational'. Best of all ask the grandchildren what they want (but which the parents have refused to give) and give just that.

BIRTHDAYS are minefields. Don't go. Your hip is playing you up (not a migraine – it's for young people and besides you've never had one before).

A very old granny is an oddity, not unlike Banquo's ghost. With your bronchitis you might accidentally blow out the candles, or ask for a goodie bag when the collecting parents come for 'the sherry'.

LOLA if you have inadvertently become an employee (school-run, babysitting, cooking and part-time nurse) do please draw up a contract. It can be part of a post-natal agreement, but more sensitive. Don't wait until the Government legislates to pay grandmothers. Charge now on principle.

DON'T GIVE ADVICE. Say they're doing a grand job but you could suggest they watch the wonderful TV programmes showing how easy it is to control the terrible twos: or give a book on 'parent induced' behavioural problems. At the same time, develop a mindset that the grandchildren are talented, very bright, artistic, sensitive, kind, pretty, and when they are with you are well adjusted and perfect.

LOLA you will inevitably be criticised. Just go home and cry, or better still cry first and then go home.

Try not to resent grandfathers. They are universally and unconditionally LOVED – doing very little – putting up the odd shelf, digging up the odd weed, playing the odd game of 'Snap', or sleeping.

Finally, LOLA, remember a grandmother is not a replica of 'mother'. You can be a 'Wow', allowing them to:- win at games (if you win they'll get bored); join in loud raucous activities; look ridiculous if they want you to dress-up or role-play; read the tea leaves – always give good news; let them experiment with your hearing aid; and the ultimate for the lucky grannies who can – TAKE YOUR TEETH OUT! You will be a granny never to be forgotten.

GO TO WORK ON YOUR EGO
SOCIALISE WITH YOUR SUPEREGO
BUT STAY AT HOME WITH YOUR ID

A simplistic but insightful modus vivendi which compartmentalises the varied complex exceptional and colourful traits that are you.

It is easy to take your conscientious, efficient and smiling EGO to work – having kissed your nearest and dearest. And very easy to leave your ID behind closed doors, to be inflicted only on your nearest and dearest.

Whereas the SUPEREGO takes you and your nearest and dearest to dancing and dinner parties where you can explain your success and fine moral fibre (you have forgiven your parents).

Curiously the EGO and ID sometimes accompany you.

Full marks. You are now free of GUILT and IN CONTROL, and you have INSIGHT – but not too much.

How to achieve this is up to you. You can Go-it-Alone by in-depth self-searching and worrying, and more worrying; meditation, yoga and advice from magazines or spurious adverts; or increase your mortgage and go for Psychoanalysis. (In order to get a good return for their money, a LOLA has to hazard a guess at life expectancy.)

Why not stay as you are? *Plus Ça Change*.

LOLITA to LOLA has been eventful.

L.O.O.L.A. (Little Old Old Lady Alone)
may be even more so.